AQA GCSE POETRY ANTHOLOGIES:

CONFLICT AND POWER

&

LOVE AND RELATIONSHIPS –

THE STUDENT GUIDE

DAVID WHEELER

Red Axe Books

ISBN: 978-0993218378

Find us at:

www.dogstailbooks.co.uk

The painting on the front cover is 'Circles' by Wassily Kandinsky

CONTENTS

Introduction

I hope you find this revision guide useful. It consists of an individual analysis of each poem in both the AQA Poetry Anthologies – Conflict and Power and also Love and Relationships. The analysis of each poem follows the same pattern: there is a section on the poet and the context in which the poem was written and some facts about each author; unfamiliar words are explained; and then each poem has a commentary which focuses on both what the poem is about and the style, form and structure that the poet uses. A final section on each poem summarizes the poem's overall impact and effect. There are no colours, few illustrations, but you will get a clear sense of what each poem is about and each poem's overall effect.

Who or what is this book for?

Perhaps you missed that crucial lesson on one particular poem that you find hard to understand? Good lessons are better than this book, because through different activities and through careful questioning and probing your teacher will help you to arrive at an understanding, an appreciation of the poem that you work out for yourself – and that process is invaluable – it's a process of thinking and exploring as a group, in a pair perhaps and as an individual, and, no matter how good the notes that your class-mates made, those notes are no substitute for having been there and gone through the process of the lesson. So, maybe, through absence, you feel a little out of touch with some of the poems: this book will help you.

Alternatively you may want to read about ideas which you have not encountered in class. Alternatively you may have the sort of teacher who allows you to respond in your own way to the poems; that is a completely valid and worthwhile approach, of course, but it does not suit every student: some students like to have clear guidelines about the meaning of what they read and to have various interpretations suggested to them so that they are at least aware of the overall gist of the poem. It still leaves you free to make up your own mind and have your own ideas, but it does provide a starting point – this book will give you that starting point.

You may be trying to revise the poems in the final days and weeks before the exam and want a quick refresher on poems that you first studied in class a long time ago; maybe it was a Friday afternoon and you weren't paying complete attention; maybe you were late for the lesson and never quite 'got' what the poem is about; maybe you were distracted by something more interesting happening outside and spent the lesson gazing out of the window. This book will help you get to grips with those poems.

It is very unlikely, but you may be reading these poems on your own for the very first time – this book will help you too, because I have assumed that you know nothing about the poem or about poetry, and the commentary on each poem is written so that you can start from scratch. Of course, some of you might find this a tiny bit condescending – and I apologize for that. I should also apologize if there are ideas in this book which are different from ones you have encountered before in class. There are as many different ways to read a poem as there are readers, and each reader might have a slightly different view of a particular poem – as we shall see. For example, most readers (pupils, teachers, professional critics) would agree that 'London' by William Blake is critical of the society he lives in; most would agree that 'London' is a bitter attack on the London that he lived in, but quite what the final verse means is open to a variety of interpretations!

So... if you want a book that tells you what each poem means; comments on features of style and structure; suggests the tone or the overall impact of each poem; gives you the necessary background knowledge to understand each poem – then this is it. At the end you will find a glossary of poetic terms, but after this introduction, there is a commentary on each poem – each commentary is self-contained and can be read on its own. Throughout the book I have used the words that I would use if I were teaching a lesson on these poems – if I use words you don't know or haven't heard, then look them up. Part of education, part of writing well about Literature is the way you yourself write, so to expand your vocabulary is a good thing. Terms which have specific literary meanings are all in the glossary at the back of the book.

Help Yourself!

I hope you find this book helpful in some ways, perhaps many ways. It deliberately does not include very detailed information about the authors for two reasons. Firstly, it would be a waste of space. Secondly, the internet is a rich source of information about writers and their work – an internet search on any of your studied poets or poems will throw up all sorts of interesting resources, including student chat boards, online revision chat-rooms as well as more obvious sources of information like Wikipedia or web sites associated with a particular author. Where there is detailed biographical information here, it is because it is vital to an understanding of the poem.

But do be warned – all the information you can possibly find about a particular poet may help to clarify something you already sensed about the poem, but it is no substitute for engagement with the poem itself. And in the examination the examiner does <u>not</u> want to read a potted biography of the poet whose poem you have chosen to write about. Besides - generalizing from what we know about a writer or his/her era is a dangerous thing: for example, it is important to be aware of William Blake's political beliefs and to be aware that he wrote 'London' during the years of the French Revolution – some might say that without such an awareness the poem cannot be fully appreciated and understood – BUT that will not help you explain the impact of individual words and lines and images at all, nor will it help you write well in the examination. Very often I have started my commentary on a poem with necessary information to help you understand it, but you don't need to reproduce all that information in the exam - it is there to help you fully understand significant details about the poem; to try to reproduce the process of discovery that a good lesson will guide you through. But it probably has little place in the examination.

You may be the sort of student who is doing English Language or English Literature because it is compulsory at your school. But it may also be that as you progress through the course you come to feel that English is a subject that you like and are good at; you may even be intrigued or fascinated by some of the poems in the anthology. If that happens, then do not rely on this book. Look on the internet for resources that will further your interest. For example, if one poet makes a special impact on you – read some of their other work; you will find a lot of it available on-line. Many of the poets in the Literary Heritage sections are now out of copyright – their work is freely available on-line. Many of the contemporary poets have their own websites which can be a fascinating source of extra information and contain links to other poems or biographical information. So there are many ways in which you can help yourself: it's a good habit to get into, especially if you start thinking about the possibility of doing English at A level.

But please remember this is no substitute for a close engagement with the poems themselves. And just as importantly – this book is no substitute for a good lesson which allows you to think about the poem's language and ideas, and then slowly come to an understanding of it. After understanding it (and that is an emotional as much as a logical understanding of it), you may come to appreciate it. What does that mean? Well, as you go through the course and read more and more poems then you may find that you prefer some to others. The next step is to identify why you prefer some poems to others: in this there are no right answers, but there are answers which are clearer and better expressed than others. And preference must be based on reasons to do with the way the poem is written or its overall emotional impact: it's your job to put what you think and feel into words – I cannot help you do that. I can merely point out some of the important features and meanings of the poems. As you grow in confidence and perhaps read other writing on these poems or listening to your teacher or your classmates, then you will start to formulate your own opinions – stealing an idea from one person, a thought from somewhere else and combining all these different things into your own view of the poem. And that is appreciation. As soon as you say you prefer one poem to another you are engaging in a critical reaction to what you have read – in exactly the same way that people prefer one film to another or one song or performer to another.

Romanticism

In this cluster of poems the first three are designated Romantic poems and it is important that you have an understanding of what Romanticism was. It has very little to do with the word 'romantic' as we apply it today to an event like Valentine's Day.

Romanticism is the name given to the artistic, political and cultural movement that emerged in England and Germany in the 1790s and in the rest of Europe in the 1820s and beyond. It was a movement that saw great changes in literature, painting, sculpture, architecture and music, and found its catalyst in the new philosophical ideas of Jean Jacques Rousseau and Thomas Paine, and in response to the American, French and industrial revolutions. Its chief emphasis was on freedom of individual self-expression, sincerity, spontaneity and originality, but it also looked to the distant past of the Middle Ages for some of its inspiration. In Romantic thought the nature of the poet changed: no longer was a poet someone who could manipulate words well and with skill; the poet was a special individual with a unique vision to communicate and with special insights to communicate through his poetry.

The key characteristics of Romantic poetry in English are:

- a reverence for and veneration of the natural world.
- a belief that the poet was a special person who had important truths to communicate and whose experiences were more intense than those of ordinary people.
- an emphasis on individualism and intense emotion.

- a increased interest in ordinary people – the rural poor and the urban working classes.
- a political radicalism, best summed up by the watchwords of the French Revolution – liberty, fraternity, equality.
- an overwhelming emphasis on the sensibility and imagination of the poet.
- an interest in medieval and ancient history.
- a veneration of Shakespeare.
- a desire to be original and to reject the orthodoxies of the immediate past.

Of course, not all the poets that we label 'Romantic' displayed all these characteristics all through their careers.

Contemporary Poetry & the Literary Heritage

You will probably have noticed that the poems within each section or cluster of your anthology are designated as Literary Heritage poems. Why? Contemporary poetry consists of poems written in the very recent past by living poets and they are here because as you study English or English Literature, it is felt to be important that you realize that poetry is not dead and poetry is not only written by dead white Englishmen: it is alive and it is being written now all over the English-speaking world by men and by women from a wide variety of backgrounds. So the contemporary poems are there to remind you that poetry is alive and well and thriving. Indeed, as I have already mentioned, many of the contemporary poets have their own websites or perform poetry readings which you may be lucky enough to attend during your course. You can also see some performances of these poems on the internet.

The poems in the first half of the anthology are generally by dead white Englishmen, although there are some poems by women. That sounds dismissive (dead white Englishmen), but it's not meant to be. They are in the anthology to remind you that writers have been writing poetry in English for hundreds of years and that what happens over those centuries is that an agreement emerges about which poems are some of the greatest or most significant ever written in the English Language. How does such agreement emerge? Well, mainly through people continuing to read the poems, responding to them and enjoying them; another concrete way is for the poems to appear in anthologies – which ensures them an even wider audience. The point you need to grasp is that writing in English poetry has been going on for hundreds of years and what has been written in the past influences what is written now. Many contemporary poets will have read the poems that you will read in the Literary Heritage sections. So when you read, for example, 'Ozymandias' by Percy Shelley for the first time, you will be joining the millions of English-speaking people all over the world who have read and enjoyed that sonnet. Organizations like the BBC have also run public votes where members of the public can vote for their favourite poem – another way that we know which poems are popular. Such poems then become part of the canon. That is not to say, however, that there is only agreement about the value of poems from the distant past: some like those by Seamus Heaney and Ted Hughes are from the closing decades of the 20th century; they are included because already there is widespread agreement that these poets are important and influential and that their poems are rewarding to read and study and enjoy.

So part of our heritage, part of the culture of speaking English, whether you speak English in Delhi or London or Manchester or Lahore or Trinidad or Liverpool or Auckland or Toronto or Cape Town or Chicago, is centuries of English poetry and a continuing poetic culture which is rich and vibrant, and includes voices from all over the English-speaking world.

The Secret of Poetry

The secret of poetry, of course, is that there is no secret. Nonetheless, I have come across lots of students who find poetry challenging or off-putting or who don't like it for some reason. I find this attitude bizarre for all sorts of reasons. But some students are very wary of poetry or turned off by it. If you are – rest assured: you shouldn't be!

Poetry is all around us: in proverbial sayings, in popular music, in the nursery rhymes we listen to or sing as children, in playground skipping chants, even in the chanting heard at football matches. All these things use the basic elements of poetry: rhythm and rhyming and very often the techniques of poetry – alliteration, repetition, word play. Advertisements and newspaper headlines also use these techniques to make what they say memorable. Ordinary everyday speech is full of poetry: if you say that something is 'as cheap as chips' you are using alliteration and a simile; if you think someone is 'two sandwiches short of a picnic', if someone is 'a pain in the arse', then you are using metaphors – the only difference is that when poets use similes and metaphors they try to use ones that are fresh and original – and memorable, in the same away that a nursery rhyme or your favourite song lyrics are memorable. Even brand names or shop names use some of the techniques of poetry: if you have a Kwik Fit exhaust supplier in your town you should note the word-play (the mis-spelling of Kwik) and the assonance – the repetition of the 'i' sound. There must be several hundred ladies' hairdressers in the UK called 'Curl Up and Dye' – which is comic word-play. You may go to 'Fat Face' because you like what they sell, but I hope that when you go next time, you'll spare a thought for the alliteration and assonance in the shop's name.

Poets also play with words. So when students tell me they don't like poetry, I don't believe them – I feel they have simply not approached it in the right way. Or perhaps not seen the link between the poetry of everyday life and the poetry they have to study and analyse for GCSE.

Poetry has been around a very long time: the earliest surviving literature in Europe consists of poetry. As far as we can tell poetry existed even before writing, and so poems were passed down by word of mouth for centuries before anyone bothered to write them down. If something is going to be passed down and remembered in this way, then it has to be memorable. And, as we shall see, poets use various techniques and tricks and patterns to make what they write easy to remember or striking in some way - just as you may remember the words to your favourite song or to a nursery rhyme that was recited to you as a small child. Let us take one example. The opening sentence of Charles Dickens' novel *A Tale of Two Cities* is

It was the best of times; it was the worst of times.

It is not poetry, but it is very memorable, because Dickens uses simple repetition, parallelism and paradox to create a very memorable sentence. Parallelism because the two halves of the sentence are the same – except for one word; and paradox because the two words – best and worst – seem to contradict each other. Now look at this recent slogan from an advert for Jaguar cars:

Don't dream it. Drive it.

This uses the same techniques as Dickens: parallelism and paradox (or juxtaposition) and it also uses alliteration. It is all about manipulating words to give them greater impact – to make them memorable.

As I am sure I will repeat elsewhere, it is always vital to read a poem aloud: your teacher might do it very well, you might be lucky enough to hear one of the living poets in the anthology read their poems aloud or you can access many recordings via the internet. I think reading a poem aloud is a good way to revise it: it has been claimed that when we read something aloud we are reading twenty times slower than when we read with our eyes – and that slowness is vital, because it allows the sound of the poem, the turn of each phrase and the rhythm of each poem to stand out. As we shall see, the way a poem sounds is absolutely crucial to its impact – for one thing, it helps you pick out techniques such as alliteration and assonance.

One of the things we will discover is that poetry is partly about pattern – patterns of sounds, of words, of rhythm; patterns of lay-out too, so that a poem and the way it is set out on the page - often separated into separate stanzas (don't call them verses) – is vital. If you quickly glance at a page from the anthology, you would probably assume that what is on the page is a poem – because we have certain expectations of the way that poems look. So what? You have probably been aware for a long time that poets often organize what they write into stanzas. For me this an absolutely crucial part of poetry because as human beings we are in love with patterns, we are addicted to patterns – and that is one of the many reasons we love poetry or find it so appealing. Patterns dominate our lives. We may have patterns on our clothes, our furnishings, our curtains, our carpets. But patterns rule our lives more completely than that: seen from above even a housing estate has patterns – the street lights at regular intervals, the garages and gardens in the same relationship to the houses; a spider's web on a frosty morning; the unique patterns of snowflakes; a honeycomb; your school uniform perhaps; the rhythm of your day, of the timetable you follow at school, of your week, of the seasons and of the year. And where patterns do not exist we like to invent them: the periodic table of elements (which you may be familiar with from Chemistry) does not exist as a table out there in nature – it's the human need to organize and give things a pattern which is responsible for the way it looks. Or look at a map of the world, criss-crossed by lines of longitude and latitude – and invented by the human mind as an aid for navigation.

What on earth has this to do with poetry? Well, poetry, especially from the past, likes to follow patterns and this structure that poets choose is something we instinctively like; it is also important when poets set up a pattern, only to break it to make whatever they are saying even more memorable because it breaks the pattern. We will see this happen in some of the poems in the anthology.

Let us look at it another way. Take the sonnet: if you choose to write a sonnet, you are committing yourself to trying to say what you want to say in 140 syllables, arranged in equal lines of 10 syllables each and fitted to a complex rhyming scheme. It is very hard to do, so why bother? Partly because it is a challenge – to force you to condense what you want to say into 140 syllables concentrates the mind and, more importantly, makes for language that can be very condensed and full of meaning. And, of course, the sonnet has been around for centuries so to choose to write one now means you are following (and hoping to bring something new and surprising) to a long-established form.

So what is poetry? *The Oxford Concise Dictionary of Literary Terms* defines it as:

Language sung, chanted, spoken, or written according to some pattern of recurrence that emphasizes the relationships between words on the basis of sound as well as sense: this pattern is almost always a rhythm or metre, which may be supplemented by rhyme or alliteration or both. All cultures have their poetry, using it for various purposes from sacred ritual to obscene insult, but it is generally employed in those utterances and writings that call for heightened intensity of emotion, dignity of expression, or subtlety of meditation. Poetry is valued for combining pleasures of sound with freshness of ideas....

Remember some of these phrases as you read this book or as you read the poems in the Anthology – which poems have intensity of emotion? Are there some which have a freshness of ideas? Or do some make you think about things more deeply (subtlety of meditation)? Perhaps there are poems which make you do all three? What can I possibly add to the Oxford Book of Literary Terms? Think of your favourite song – whatever type of music you listen to. The song's lyrics will share many of the characteristics of poetry, but the words will be enhanced by the music and the delivery of the vocalist. Is it a song that makes you happy or sad? Angry or mellow? Whatever it makes you feel, a song takes you on an emotional journey – and that is what poems do too, except they lack musical accompaniment. So think of a poem as being like a song – designed to make you feel a particular emotion and think particular thoughts; like some songs, the emotions, the thoughts, may be quiet complex and hard to explain but the similarity is there. And that is another reason why it is important to hear the poems read aloud – they are designed to be listened to, not simply read. Short poems like the ones in the Anthology are often called lyric poems – and that is because hundreds of years ago they would have been accompanied by music. Before 1066 Anglo-Saxon bards telling even long narrative poems used to accompany themselves on a lyre – a primitive type of guitar and up to Elizabethan times lyric poems were set to music and performed.

Making Connections

As you can see from what is written above, a lot of the work in English on the Anthology is about making connections – the exam question will explicitly ask you to do this. As you study the Anthology or read this book you should try to make connections for yourself. Free your mind and make unusual connections. You might feel that some poems take you on a similar emotional journey; some poems might use metaphor or personification in similar ways; some poems were written at the same time as others and are connected by their context.

If you can connect poems because of their written style or something like structure or technique, then that will impress the examiner more than if you simply connect them by subject matter. The poems are already connected by simply being in the Anthology, so to start an answer, for example, by stating that two poems are about 'Conflict' is a waste of words. You should try to do some thinking for yourself as you read this book and reflect on the poems in the anthology– because it is a good habit to get into and helps prepare you mentally for the exam.

Do you have a favourite word? If you do, you might like to think about why you like it so much. It may well have something to do with the meaning, but it might also have something to do with the sound. Of course, some words are clearly onomatopoeic like *smash*, *bang* and *crack*. But other words have sound qualities too which alter the way we react to them – and they are not obviously onomatopoeic. For example, the word *blister* sounds quite harsh because the letter *b* and the combination of *st* sound a little unpleasant; and, of course, we know what a *blister* is and it is not a pleasant thing. On the other hand, words like *fearful* or *gentle* or *lightly* have a lighter, more delicate sound because of the letters from which they are made. Words like *glitter* and *glisten* cannot be onomatopoeic: onomatopoeia is all about imitating the sound that something makes and *glitter* and *glisten* refer to visual phenomena, but the *gl* at the start and the *st* and *tt* in the middle of the words make them sound entirely appropriate, just right, don't they?

Think of it another way: just reflect on the number of swear words or derogatory terms in English which start with *b* or *p*: *bloody, bugger, bastard, plonker, pratt, prick, prawn* – the list goes on and on. The hard *c* sound in a word like *cackle* is also unpleasant to the ear. So what? Well, as you read poems try to be aware of this, because poets often choose light, gentle sounds to create a gentle atmosphere: listen to the sounds. Of course, the meaning of the word is the dominant element that we respond to, but listen to it as well.

You don't need to know anything about the history of the English language to get a good grade at GCSE. However, where our language comes from makes English unique. English was not spoken in the British Isles until about 450 CE when tribes from what is now Holland invaded as the Roman Empire gradually collapsed. The language these tribes spoke is now known as Old English – if you were to see some it would look very foreign to your eyes, but it is where our basic vocabulary comes from. A survey once picked out the hundred words that are most used in written English: ninety-nine of them had their roots in Old English; the other one was derived from French. The French the Normans spoke had developed from Latin and so when we look at English vocabulary – all the words that are in the dictionary – we can make a simple distinction between words that come from Old English and words that come from Latin – either directly from Latin or from Latin through French. [I am ignoring for the moment all the hundreds of thousands of words English has adopted from all the other languages in the world.]

So what? I hear you think. Well, just as the sounds of words have different qualities, so do the words derived from Old English and from Latin. Words that are Old English in origin are short, blunt and down-to-earth; words derived from Latin or from Latin through French are generally longer and sound more formal. Take a simple example: house, residence, domicile. *House* comes from Old English; *residence* from Latin through French and *domicile* direct from Latin. Of course, if you invited your friends round to your residence, they would probably think you were sounding rather fancy – but that is the whole point. We associate words of Latinate origin with formality and elegance and sometimes poets might use words conscious of the power and associations that they have. Where a poet has used largely Latinate vocabulary it creates a special effect and there are poems in the Anthology where I have pointed this feature out. Equally, the down to earth simplicity of words of English origin can be robust and strong.

Alliteration is a technique that is easy to recognize and is used by many poets and writers to foreground their work. It can exist, of course, in any language. However, it seems to have appealed to writers in English for many centuries. Before 1066 when the Normans invaded and introduced French customs and culture, poetry was widely written in a language we now call Old English, or Anglo Saxon. Old English poetry did not rhyme. How was it patterned then? Each line had roughly the same number of syllables, but what was more important was that each line had three or four words that alliterated. Alliterative poetry continued to be written in English until the 14th century and if you look at these phrases drawn from everyday English speech I think you can see that it has a power even today: busy as a bee, cool as a cucumber, good as gold, right as rain, cheap as chips, dead as a doornail, kith and kin, hearth and home, spick and span, hale and hearty. Alliteration can also be found in invented names. Shops: Coffee Corner, Sushi Station, Caribou Coffee, Circuit City. Fictional characters: Peter Pan, Severus Snape, Donald Duck, Mickey Mouse, Nicholas Nickleby, Humbert Humbert, King Kong, Peppa Pig. The titles of films and novels: *Pride and Prejudice, Sense and Sensibility, Debbie Does Dallas, House on Haunted Hill, Gilmour Girls, V for Vendetta, A Christmas Carol, As Good as it Gets, The Witches of Whitby, The Wolf of Wall Street.* Alliteration is an easy way to make words and phrases memorable.`

So what? Well, as you read the poems and see alliteration being used, I think it is helpful to bear in mind that alliteration is not some specialized poetic technique, but is part of the fabric of everyday English too and it is used in everyday English for the same reasons that it is used by poets – to make the words more memorable.

An Approach to Poetry

This next bit may only be relevant if you are studying the poems for the first time and it is an approach that I use in the classroom. It works well and helps students get their bearing when they first encounter a poem. These are the Five Ws. They are not my idea, but I use them in the classroom all the time. They are simply five questions which are a starting point, a way of getting into the poem and a method of approaching an understanding of it. With some poems some of the answers to the questions are more important than others; with some poems these questions and our answers to them will not get us very far at all – but it is where we will start. I will follow this model with each commentary. They are also a good way to approach the unseen poem. The five questions to ask of each poem you read are:

- Who?

- When?

- Where?

- What?

- Why?

WHO? Who is in the poem? Whose voice the poem uses? This is the first and most basic question. In many poems the poet speaks as themselves, but sometimes they are ventriloquists – they pretend to be someone else. So first of all we must identify the voice of the poem. We must ask ourselves to whom the poem is addressed. It isn't always right to say – the reader; some poems are addressed to a particular individual. And, of course, there may well be other people mentioned in the poem itself. Some poetry is quite cryptic, so who 'you' and 'they' are in a poem make a crucial difference to the way we interpret it. Why are poems 'cryptic'? Well, one reason is that they use language in a very compressed way – compressed perhaps because of the length of each line or the decision to use rhyme.

WHEN? When was the poem written and when is it set? This is where context is important. We know our context: we are reading the poem now, but when the poem was written and when the poem is set (not always the same, by any means) is crucial to the way we interpret it. The gender or background of the poet might be important, the society they were living in, the circumstances which led them to write the poem – all these things can be crucial to how we interpret the poem.

WHERE? Where is the poem set? Where do the events described in the poem take place? With some poems this question is irrelevant; with others it is absolutely vital – it all depends on the poem. In the Anthology you will find some poems which depend on some understanding of where they are set for them to work; you will find other poems where the location is not specified or is irrelevant or generalized – again it depends on the poem.

WHAT? This means what happens in a poem. Some poems describe a place; some describe a particular moment in time; some tell a story; some have a story buried beneath their surface; some make statements – some may do several or all of these things at once. They are all potentially different, but what happens is something very basic and should be grasped before you can move on to really appreciate a poem. Very often I have kept this section really short, because it is only when you start to look closely at language that you fully understand what is going on.

WHY? This is the hardest question of all and the one with a variety of possible answers, depending on your exact view of the poem in question. I like to think of it as asking ourselves 'Why did the poet write this poem?' Or 'What is the overall message or emotional impact of this poem?' To answer it with every poem, we need to look at all the other questions, the way the poet uses language and its effect on us, and try to put into words the tone of the voice of the poem and the poem's overall impact. Students in the classroom often seem puzzled by my asking them to discuss the poem's tone. But it boils down to this - if you were reading the poem out loud, what tone of voice would you use? What is the mood or atmosphere of the poem? Does the poet, or whoever the poet is pretending to be, have a particular attitude to what he or she is writing about? Answering these questions helps us discuss the tone of the poem. But you may not agree with everybody else about this and this is good: through disagreement and discussion, our understanding of what we read is sharpened. In the commentaries on each poem in this Anthology this question 'Why?' is answered at the very end of each commentary, because it is only after looking closely at the poet's use of language, form and structure that we can begin to answer it. If you feel you know the poem well enough, you might just use the section 'Why?' for each poem as a quick reminder of what its main message is. For all the poems the 'Why?' section consists of a series of bullet points which attempt to give you the words to express what the poem's main point is.

A Word of Warning

This book and the commentaries on individual poems that follow are full of words to do with literature – the technical devices such as metaphor, simile, oxymoron. These are the vocabulary to do with the craft of writing and it is important that you understand them and can use them with confidence. It is the same as using the word *osmosis* in Biology or *isosceles* in Maths. However, in the examination, it is absolutely pointless to pick out a technique unless you can say something vaguely intelligent about its effect – the effect is vital! The examiner will know when a poet is using alliteration and does not need you to point it out; the sort of writing about poetry that consists of picking out technical devices and saying nothing about their effect or linking them in some meaningful way to the subject matter is worthless. I will suggest, in each commentary, what the effect might be, but we can generalize and say that all techniques with words are about making the poem memorable in some away – and this 'making something memorable' is also about foregrounding language. Language that is foregrounded means that it is different from normal everyday language and that it draws attention to itself by being different – it would be like if we all went round every day and tried to use a metaphor and alliteration in everything that we said or if we tried speaking in rhyme all day – people would notice!

Warming Up

Before we look at any of the poems from the anthology, I want to briefly examine two poems to give you a taste of the approach that will be followed throughout the rest of the book. So we will start by looking at two completely different poems. I am not going to subject either to a full analysis, but I will demonstrate with both poems some crucial ways of reading poetry and give you some general guidance which will stand you in good stead when we deal with the poems in the anthology itself. This is not meant to confuse you, but to help. I cannot stress enough that these two poems are not ones that you will be assessed on. They are my choice – and I would use the same method in the classroom – introducing a class very slowly to poetry and 'warming up' for the anthology by practising the sorts of reading skills which will help with any poem. Besides, you may find the method valuable in your preparation for answering on the unseen poem in the exam.

The first poem we will consider is one of the most famous poems in the English Language – Sonnet 116 by William Shakespeare:

SONNET 116

Let me not to the marriage of true minds
Admit impediments. Love is not love

Which alters when it alteration finds,
Or bends with the remover to remove:
O no; it is an ever-fixed mark,
That looks on tempests, and is never shaken;
It is the star to every wandering bark,
Whose worth's unknown, although his height be taken.
Love's not Time's fool, though rosy lips and cheeks
Within his bending sickle's compass come;
Love alters not with his brief hours and weeks,
But bears it out even to the edge of doom.
   If this be error and upon me proved,
   I never writ, nor no man ever loved.

Context

Shakespeare is the most famous writer England has ever produced and his plays are known throughout the world. 'Sonnet 116' by William Shakespeare is part of a sonnet sequence of 154 sonnets – also known as a sonnet cycle. Readers have commented that in the sonnets as a whole, Shakespeare covers every aspect of arguably the most important and strongest human emotion – love - as well as our most powerful instinct – sexual desire and the whole range of what happens in what we now call human relationships. Unlike Shakespeare's plays (most of which were unpublished during his lifetime), the sonnets were published in 1609. What does this tell us? We are not entirely sure: it is generally felt that it shows that poetry was held in higher regard than writing plays, so perhaps Shakespeare published the sonnets to achieve fame and wealth; there is also the fact that in Shakespeare's era there were no copyright laws – so once a play was published, there was nothing to stop any theatre putting a play on without giving the writer any performance fees.

Of the 154 sonnets some are very famous and appears in many anthologies. These very famous ones are well-known by the general public too: in the past, BBC Radio 4 has sometimes run public surveys to discover the nation's favourite poem or the nation's favourite love poem and Shakespeare's sonnets are frequently voted into the top ten. If you like 'Sonnet 116', then you might like to read some of his others. They are readily available on-line and are known by their number and the first line:

Sonnet 18 – Shall I compare thee to a summer's day?

Sonnet 29 – When in disgrace with Fortune and men's eyes

Sonnet 55 – Not marble or the gilded monuments

Sonnet 57 – Being your slave what should I do?

Sonnet 71 – No longer mourn for me when I am dead

Sonnet 91 – Some glory in their birth, some in their skill

Sonnet 129 – The expense of spirit in a waste of shame

Sonnet 130 – My mistress' eyes are nothing like the sun

Because so little is known about Shakespeare's private life, there has been endless speculation about who the sonnets are addressed to – but none of this speculation helps us get any closer to the individual sonnets and their meaning and impact. Personally I find it of no interest whatsoever, because for me the words are what make the sonnets memorable and worth reading now – over four hundred years since they were first published.

'Sonnet 116' is often used in modern marriage services (nowadays some churches allow couples considerable freedom in choosing some of the words they use during the service) and I have even seen cards for sale which reproduce the words of the sonnet – these cards are intended to be sent to people who are getting married. The whole sonnet presents a love that is steadfast and loyal and unchanging in the face of other changes. We will look closely at the language and tone of the sonnet, but also consider a deeper and darker interpretation.

impediments – obstacles.

or...remove – or ends when one person leaves or stops the relationship.

ever-fixèd – permanent, not moving.

bark – ship.

time's fool – the fool of time, subject to time and aging.

bending sickle – a scythe and its curved shape; the Grim Reaper carries a sickle; sickles an scythes are long-handled tools used for chopping down tall crops or weeds; here it is used metaphorically – Time chops us down because we succumb to age and finally death.

compass – range.

bears it out – endures it.

doom – Doomsday, the end of the world in Christian mythology, the day of Final Judgement when Christ will come to earth again and decide who goes to Heaven and who to Hell. Shakespeare uses this to suggest that love will last forever – until the end of time or the end of the world.

Who? The voice of the poet – but the commentary that follows suggests the implied presence of other people.

When? The sonnets were published in 1609, but most scholars believe that Shakespeare began to write them in the 1590s. Within the poem no particular time is specified.

Where? No particular place is specified, so the location does not seem important.

What? Shakespeare states that true love will never change and then explores this assertion through a series of images in order to prove or demonstrate that love will never change.

Commentary

The opening sentence of the sonnet is justly famous: the recurrence of the letter *m* which both alliterates and is within certain words and the way the first line runs on into the second

Let me not to the marriage of true minds

Admit impediments

creates a gentle, calm, mellifluous tone which is appropriate to the sense: assonance on the letter *l* allows creates euphony, which is all enhanced by the enjambment. The next sentence too

Love is not love

Which alters when it alteration finds.

is often quoted on its own and offered as a universal truth: true love never changes no matter what happens. This second sentence is memorable not just because of the sentiment but because of the words: the repetition of the word *love* as well as *alter/alteration* and the soft sounds of the letter *l* and *w* and *f.* So far the sonnet is quite clearly concerned with marriage and *alters* is a pun on what we find at the eastern end of a church the altar. *Impediment* too is a word, a very important word, in the Church of England marriage service. In the marriage service the priest says to the congregation, before the couple exchange their vows of marriage:

Does anyone know of any just cause or impediment why these two should not be joined together in holy matrimony?

Impediment here means an obstacle. At this point in the service, centuries ago, this was the moment when someone in the congregation could mention an obstacle – such one of the couple being already married or promised to someone else or below the legal age to marry or whatever. The final line of the quatrain continues this pattern of repetition – *remover/remove.*

The second quatrain introduces new images in an effort to define what love is. Line 5 begins with a dramatic exclamation – *O no* – and then introduces a metaphor based on ships and navigation. Love is *ever-fixèd*: it never changes and can endure the fury of tempests without being shaken; love is like a star that guides sailors who would otherwise be lost (*wandering*) and they measure the height of the star (love) even before they understand whether the star will help them navigate. Shakespeare uses assonance – *star* assonates with the rhyme words *bark* and *mark* – and *whose worth's unknown* – repeats the same sound with *o* – which alos goes back to the exclamation at the start of the quatrain. This creates a sort of aural harmony even though he is writing about potentially dangerous things – tempests, and ships that are lost.

The third quatrain changes the line of thought again. It starts with a bold statement – *Love's not Time's fool*; Shakespeare means that true love will not alter even though time changes our physical appearance as we age. Time destroys *rosy lips and cheeks*. Not the consonance on *c* in *sickle's compass come*. Line 11 deliberately echoes the opening quatrain with its use of *alters*. The whole quatrain is held together not just by sense and subject matter and rhyme, but also alliteration – *bending, brief, but bears*. The final line says that love will last until Doomsday, the end of time.

The sonnet ends with an assertive couplet. Shakespeare states that if he is wrong – that if love is impermanent or transitory then it follows that he, the poet, never wrote a word and no human being ever really loved.

This poem is usually read as a definition of love or true love: an emotion that survives time and tempests, that will never change, no matter what happens. This is why it is so popular in connection with marriages – it serves, people think, as a vow of love that will last forever. Perhaps its power has a lot to do with its sounds: we have noted the clever use of repetition; the euphony created by the soft consonants in the opening quatrain; and, perhaps, its appeal has something to do with Shakespeare's straightforward imagery of stars and ships, rosy cheeks, death personified with his bending sickle. However, a closer reading will show that there is another possibility, another way to interpret this very famous poem.

Remember that in the first sentence Shakespeare had said he was not going to admit impediments – he is going to say nothing at this point of the marriage service. This suggests that Shakespeare is writing about the marriage of someone else and asserting that he still loves that person and his love will never change, despite the fact that they are marrying someone else and not him. It is ironic, isn't it, that the sonnet is so often used in marriage services: this is a poem about the end of a relationship – a relationship that is ending because one of the people involved in the relationship is getting married. Consequently, the speaker's feelings are of sadness and a sense of betrayal, but they are controlled by the strict form of the sonnet which helps to restrain the terrible sadness the speaker feels.

In the light of this reading of the poem, the poem's imagery still fits with what I wrote earlier in the summary, but some of the images take on a darker, sadder tone and atmosphere. The simile involving the *wandering bark* works as a simile, but it might also suggest Shakespeare's emotional state now that his former lover has rejected him to marry someone else – he is like a ship drifting. Love that bears it out until the edge of doom, means a love that will never die and will keep going until Doomsday, but that word *doom* perhaps suggests the terrible sadness that Shakespeare feels at the end of the relationship: in a sense it is almost like the end of the world for him. *Bears it out* suggests a determination to keep going despite the heartbreak he feels – and he does, in a sense, keep going, because the sonnet reaches its conclusion.

Why?

This world-famous poem

- offers a definition of love which many readers have comforting and inspiring.

- asserts that true love lasts forever and will endure absence and time and even death.

- uses simple repetition and wonderfully crafted combinations of sound to create euphony.

BUT it might also be read as

- a poem full of heartbreak and sadness at the loss of a loved one who marries someone else.

Here is the second poem that we will look at as an unseen:

The Sick Rose

O rose, thou art sick!
  The invisible worm,
That flies in the night,
  In the howling storm,

Has found out thy bed   5
  Of crimson joy,
And his dark secret love
  Does thy life destroy

thou – you

thy - your

Who? The voice of the poet, the invisible worm, a rose.

When? In the night during a storm.

Where? Hard to say... in the bed of the rose.

What? Just using what we know from the poem, we can say that an invisible worm discovers the dark secret love of the rose and destroys it during a storm.

It is obvious that this method will not get us very far with this type of poem or, at least, will not get us beyond a superficial interpretation of what it means. Before you read any further, please take the time to read my comments below about William Blake's poem 'London' on page 40, because Blake is also the author of 'The Sick Rose'.

What can we say with any certainty about this poem? Its mood is sinister. It is night-time and there is a howling storm. An invisible worm has found out where the rose has its bed and is coming to take its life. *Found out* suggests that the bed needs to be hidden. Paradoxically, although the worm is going to destroy the life of the rose, the worm has a *dark secret love* for the rose: this is now especially disturbing – a love which is dark and secret and which is destructive of life. Not only is it night and, therefore, dark, but the love of the worm is also dark and secret and destructive. We expect love to be a positive emotion which brings good things to our lives.

When faced with this poem many readers want to interpret the poem symbolically – otherwise it becomes a poem about horticulture. The poem is full of words that we associate with love - *rose, bed, joy, love.* In addition, in our culture sending someone roses, especially red roses, is a token of love. But this is a love which has gone wrong and is destructive. Many readers also find the shape of the worm rather phallic – suggestive of the penis. Think of all the types of love which might be considered 'wrong' or destructive. This is the list I came up with, but I am sure you can think of many others:

- Love for someone who does not love you back.

- Love for someone who is already married or in a relationship.

- Love which cannot be expressed.

- Love that transmits disease through unprotected sex.

- Love between two people from different religions.

- Love which is against the law.

- Love which is unwanted by the person you love.

- Love between two people of different class backgrounds.

- Love between two people of the same gender.

- Love or sexual expressions of love which are condemned by the church or by religious doctrine or law.

- Love which is possessive and selfish.

The point of this list is really to show that Blake's power of compression suggests a love that has gone wrong and leaves us to interpret it. To say that 'The Sick Rose' is about any one of the situations listed above would be totally wrong; to say that it suggests them all and encompasses them all, suggests the power of Blake's writing.

If you have read 'London' and if you remember that the rose is the national symbol of England, then this poem becomes even more than a poem about love gone wrong – it becomes (perhaps) a poem about the state of England and a warning that it will soon be destroyed. You don't have to identify exactly what or who the worm is – the poem does that for you: the worm is destructive and capable of killing – it is a symbol of ALL the things Blake hated in his society. Blake's point is that the rose is sick and is about to be destroyed by sinister, invisible powers.

Finally, if you need any proof of Blake's power to compress meaning, just look at how many words I have used in an attempt to give meaning to his words: Blake uses (including the title) only thirty-seven! This is part of the poem's power and art – that is uses powerful words and imagery from which we can extract a multitude of meanings.

Why? This astonishingly compressed and darkly evocative poem is

- a protest about the England that Blake lived in.

- a protest about the way the church and society saw certain types of love as wrong.

- a warning that love – or what we call love- can be destructive if it is not fulfilled.

- a plea for tolerance and inclusion for those who conventional morality condemns.

Endings

This may seem like an obvious point, one hardly worth drawing attention to, but you have seen from the poems discussed above that the endings of poem are absolutely vital and crucial to their overall effect. In 'The Sick Rose' the final word – *destroy* – carries threat and menace. You will find in many of the poems in the Anthology the ending – the final stanza, the final line, the final sentence, even sometimes the final word – changes what has gone before and forces us to see things differently. So be aware of this as you read and as you revise. When you are writing about poems, the way they end and the emotional conclusion they achieve is a simple way to compare and contrast them. It may not be easy to express what it is exactly that they do achieve, but make sure you write something about the endings, because the endings are often the key to the whole poem. Remember – a poem (like a song) is an emotional journey and the destination, the ending, is part of the overall message, probably its most important part.

CONFLICT & POWER

'Ozymandias' – Percy Shelley

Context

Percy Bysshe Shelley was born in 1792 and drowned in a boating accident just before his 30th birthday in 1822. He lived in turbulent times: the French Revolution had begun in 1789 and in Britain the Industrial Revolution was changing the country in deep and lasting ways. Shelley was quite a rebel – and was a political radical. He sympathized with the ideas behind the French Revolution and wanted to see greater change in Britain – more democracy, more freedom, less oppression. You should remember that although Britain was an enormously wealthy nation (because of the Industrial Revolution and the huge expanse of the British Empire), the majority of the population lived in appalling poverty and most adults did not have the vote – the right to vote was limited to those who owned a certain amount of property and was, therefore, limited to a tiny minority of adult males. It was not until 1928 that all men (regardless of what they owned) were able to vote.

'Ozymandias' by Percy Shelley is one of his best-known poems, although, as we shall see, not very typical of his work. Shelley was a political radical which meant that he felt the England of his day was repressive and unfair and was in great need of political reform. He was very conscious of the massive gap between which and poor, the lack of real democracy (most men and no women had the vote) and the terrible conditions of the workers in the factories that had sprung up as a result of the Industrial Revolution. Britain was the first country in the world to have an industrial revolution and, with the British Empire also growing and expanding at the same time, Britain was an enormously rich and powerful country – the leading superpower of the day (especially after 1815 when the Duke of Wellington defeated Napoleon and the French at the Battle of Waterloo). However, this enormous wealth was concentrated in the hands of the rich and powerful. The mass of the population lived in conditions of great poverty. In most of his poems Shelley is very open and explicit about his feelings of hatred and anger towards the government of his day; in that sense 'Ozymandias' is less typical because it takes a very long historical perspective and makes no mention of contemporary politics or political leaders.

Ozymandias is another name for Rameses II who was the king of Egypt in the 13th century BCE – over three thousand years ago. The king clearly commissioned a sculptor to carve a statue of him with the inscription 'Look on my works, ye Mighty, and despair'. Why would such a powerful ruler commission such a statue? So that his power and rule will be remembered forever. However, this has not happened. All that remains of the statue are *two vast and trunkless legs of stone.* Nearby *half-sunk* in the sand is part of his head, buried by the sands of time. The point of the poem is that for all Rameses' power and his arrogant assumption that he would be remembered because of this huge statue, the statue has been destroyed by time.

A little known fact is that, in a spirit of friendly rivalry, Shelley wrote 'Ozymandias' in an informal competition with another writer Horace Smith. Below is Smith's version. You will see, that Smith's poem touches on the same themes as Shelley's, but is a little more chilling in its depiction of a future London through which a hunter wanders, trying to make sense of the ruins of what was once British civilization. Shelley's poem lacks that explicit warning for the political rulers of his day –

although you could say it is implied. Interestingly, at the time, Smith's poem was considered better. You can judge for yourself. Here is Smith's poem, also called 'Ozymandias' originally.

In Egypt's sandy silence, all alone,

Stands a gigantic leg, which far off throws

The only shadow that the desert knows:

'I am the great Ozymandias,' saith the stone,

'The King of Kings, this mighty city shows

The wonders of my hand.' The City's gone –

Nought but the leg remaining to disclose

The site of this forgotten Babylon.

We wonder – and some hunter may express

Wonder like ours, when through the wilderness

Where London stood, holding the wolf in chase,

He meets some fragment huge, and stops to guess

What powerful but unrecorded race

Once dwelt in that annihilated place.

It is part of the mystery of the canon that Shelley's poem is so well-known, but that Smith's is hardly ever re-printed. Which do you prefer? I quite like the last line of Smith's because of his use of the word *annihilated* – it also stresses the point of both poems more forcefully, you might argue, because it brings home to the contemporary reader the idea that even British civilization may one day crumble and become a wilderness (think of what we know about Britain's status in the world at that time) and the British become an *unrecorded race*.

antique – ancient.

trunkless legs – the trunk is the main part of the body, containing the stomach and rib cage. It has disappeared – only the legs are left.

visage – face.

Who? The narrator of the poem meets a traveller who tells him what he has seen in the desert.

When? The poem was first published in 1818.

Where? London, but the antique traveller talks of ruins of a statue seen in Egypt.

What? The traveller tells the poet about some ruins he has seen in Egypt.

Commentary

'Ozymandias' is a Petrarchan sonnet named after Rameses II who died in 1234 BCE. The narrator of the poem recounts a conversation he has had with a traveller from an antique land. The final 13 lines of the poem quote what the traveller told Shelley. In the desert the traveller has found the remains of a statue of Rameses II. All that is left are

Two vast and trunkless legs of stone

The head of the statue is lying nearby half-covered in sand. It is still possible to discern aspects of Rameses's face: the *frown*, the *sneer of cold command* which tell us he was an autocratic and authoritarian ruler. We are told that the sculptor understood those aspects of Rameses' character – the vanity and pride, the evil and unpleasant characteristics of a man used to complete power and total obedience from his subjects.

In the sestet Shelley explores the fate of such vanity and pride. Despite the often-quoted inscription

Look on my Works, ye Mighty, and despair

nothing beside remains but ruin and devastation — a *colossal wreck*. There is a double irony: both Ozymandias and the unnamed sculptor share the same fate — neither the ruler nor the sculptor nor the statue remain in any shape to prove Ozymandias's boast of power and authority. Here, I think, we can see the point of telling the story second-hand. We are reading a poem written by a man who had a conversation with someone who had been to the desert and seen the ruins of the statue: this distancing serves to diminish Ozymandias still further. These are second-hand words reported to us by the poet. This distancing effect helps to stress Ozyamndias's obscurity even more.

This sonnet is remarkable for the spare and stark imagery which the poet uses. There are lots of words which suggest solitude and decay — *trunkless, half-sunk, shattered, decay, wreck* -and so in the monotonous wastes of the desert — the traveller, the poet and then the reader encounter this ruined monument to earthly power and arrogance. We might be shocked by the ravages of time which the statue has suffered, but we end up mocking the presumptuous self-centredness and self-importance of Rameses II — and, by extension, of all autocratic rulers.

Shelley gives aural unity to the poem by the use of alliteration in the octave — *said, stone ,stand, sand, sunk, shatter'd, sneer, sculptor, survive.* In line 8 he uses parallelism

The hand that mocked them and the heart that fed.

Lines 10 and 11 are the words of Ozymandias which ring very hollow given the destruction of the statue and the decay of his civilization. Line 12 begins

Nothing beside remains.

The strong caesura here emphasizes even more the fact that the statue is wrecked and Ozymandias's arrogant boast has come to nothing. The caesura makes the line stop short and briefly end — just as Ozymandias's power stopped short when he was dead. Line 13 ends with memorable alliteration – *boundless and bare*, while the final line returns the whole sonnet to the power of nature

The lone and level sands stretch far away.

An amazing line – the double alliteration *lone/level* and *sands/stretch* followed by the assonance on the long *a* sounds in *and*, *sands* and *far away* not only make it memorable, but also remind us of the isolation and barrenness of the desert. The word 'level' is full of political significance. Because of the huge class differences in Western Europe at the time, political radicals wanted more equality so that people were on the same level: so one simple word that describes the desert also has important political ramifications.

On the one hand, this sonnet was a message to the rulers of Britain in Shelley's time: he disagreed violently with the government's policies. On the other hand, it is a more timeless message for all humanity: civilizations fall and crumble, eroded by time and nature. It is interesting that the words of the inscription have survived: perhaps Shelley is stressing that words – the words of poets, for example – will outlive dictators and tyrants.

Conflict and Power

Centuries ago Ozymandias wielded great power and control over his own kingdom. His power was so great that he caused his statues of himself to be built to demonstrate his power over his people, and the words on the pedestal are full of haughty pride and arrogance:

'My name is Ozymandias, king of kings,

Look on my works, ye Mighty, and despair!'

However, the erosion of the weather and the passage of time have both caused the statue to crumble and break up – showing his boast of absolute power to be empty and futile. Shelley is also implying – given all we know about his radical political beliefs – that the autocratic rulers of Great Britain in 1818, despite their pride and arrogance and their repressive policies– are destined ultimately for the same oblivion as Ozymandias.

A Romantic Poem?

'Ozymandias' can be seen as a typical Romantic poem because of its political stance and its awareness of the power of nature. Shelley uses the sonnet form – a traditional and highly literary form: the Romantics generally liked and admired the sonnet as practised by Shakespeare and Milton, and the form had been relatively neglected in the 18th century, so the Romantic poets felt they were reclaiming a great 'lost' poetic form. If you have read a sonnet before, it is likely it had romantic love as its subject, but John Milton had, in the 17th century, written many sonnets dealing with political issues and current events.

Why?

In this justly-famous sonnet Shelley want to show

- that human beings will all be swept away by the power of time.

- that Ozymandias, the sculptor, the traveller and Shelley himself all face the inevitability of death –*the bare and boundless sands.*

- that the hubristic pride of rulers such as Ozymandias is wrong and will not survive.

- that there is a message in all of this to the autocratic rulers of England in Shelley's own era.

- words and language can survive the destructive power of time.

'London' – William Blake

Context

William Blake (1757 – 1827) is now seen as the foremost artist and poet of his time, but his work was largely unknown during his lifetime. He was a painter as well as a poet and you can see some of his paintings in art galleries like Tate Britain in London or the Fitzwilliam Museum in Cambridge. 'London' comes from a collection called *Songs of Innocence and of Experience* which appeared together for the first time in 1794. *The Songs of Innocence* (which originally appeared on their own in 1789) are positive in tone and celebrate unspoilt nature, childhood and love. *The Songs of Experience* (from which 'London' comes) depict a corrupt society in which the prevailing mood is one of despair and in which children are exploited and love is corrupted.

This poem is often read as a profound criticism of the society Blake lived in. Everything in London is owned (*chartered*) - even the River Thames which is a natural force which one might expect to be free. Blake was writing at a time when Britain was the wealthiest country in the world because of its global empire and because of the Industrial Revolution which produced goods which were exported all over the world. But not everyone shared in this enormous wealth; the gap between rich and poor was huge, with the poor suffering really terrible living and working conditions. This poem first 'appeared' (this term will be explained below) in 1794. The date of publication is crucial: Blake is partly seeing London in this way because of events in France. In 1789 the French Revolution began, changing French society forever and ushering in a new age of freedom, equality and brotherhood. Many English people saw what was happening in France and thought it was good to have a society based on greater equality; they looked critically at British society and saw appalling inequalities and injustices. For example, you may be aware that this was the period in British history that some people campaigned against slavery in the British Empire: what is less well-known is that forms of slavery existed in London. There are recorded cases of parents selling their sons to master chimneysweeps in London. The life of a chimney sweep was likely to be short: they were sent up the chimneys of large houses to clean them. Some suffocated; others were trapped in the confined space and died; sometimes their masters would light fires below them to encourage them to work faster – they sometimes were burnt alive. For those who survived, their health was affected: they suffered from terrible lung complaints as a result of breathing in coal dust and, because of poor hygiene, might also succumb to testicular cancer brought on by the accumulated layers of biting coal dust.

Blake had produced *Songs of Innocence* on its own in 1789, although we can tell from his surviving notebooks that he always intended to write *Songs of Experience*. I have used the term 'appeared' because they were not published in a conventional sense. Blake produced each copy of *Songs of*

Innocence and of Experience at home by hand and copies were then given to friends and acquaintances. Part of this was Blake's own choice, but we can easily see that his views about Britain and its government would have been highly controversial, so open publication of them may have led to charges of sedition or treason. The British government at the time were terrified of a revolution here, like the one in France, and were doing everything they could to silence people like Blake who were critical of the society in which they lived.

Blake earned his living as an engraver. Before photographs and modern ways of reproducing images, engravings were the cheapest and easiest way of illustrating a book. Blake produced illustrations for other people's books throughout his life – that was how he earned a living. To create an engraving, the engraver has to carve, with a specialist knife, lines on a metal plate; when the plate is then covered in ink and pressed on paper the lines appear on the paper.

On page 41 you can see (in black and white) Blake's illustration for 'London'. The overall impression is of darkness, which is appropriate given the poem. However, a shaft of light illuminates a young boy who is apparently leading an old and infirm man using a crutch to walk. It comes across as an example of kindness and empathy which works a against the gloom of the poem and perhaps can therefore be seen as a symbol of hope

Blake used the same technique for reproducing his own poems. After coating the metal plate with ink and producing the outline, Blake coloured each page of each copy of *Songs of Innocence and of Experience* by hand with water colour paint. It is estimated that only 25 copies were produced in his lifetime. If you go to the British Museum you can see one copy: it is tiny and exquisitely detailed and, of course, very personal, because Blake coloured it by hand himself. In addition, to produce his poems in this way was time-consuming and arduous, since in order for the words to appear the right way round when the page was printed, they had to be written in mirror hand-writing on the plate – a painstaking process that must have taken hours and shows not only Blake's artistry, but also his devotion to hard work.

Charter'd – owned. A charter was a legal document proving possession.

mark – to notice.

marks – signs.

ban – a government edict banning people from doing something.

manacles – handcuffs or leg-irons.

hapless – unlucky.

harlot – prostitute.

marriage hearse – an oxymoron; Blake juxtaposes the idea of death (hearses carry the dead body to the graveyard) with life – marriage often produces children.

Who? The narrator recounts what he sees in the first stanza and in the next three stanzas what he hears as he wanders around London. The poem is written in the present tense which gives it an immediacy and greater impact.

When? 1794.

Where? London.

What? The narrator sees and hears a population suffering and full of pain and despair.

Commentary

The poem's narrator wanders through the streets of London looking at the suffering of his fellow citizens which is apparent on their faces. The first stanza concentrates on what he sees; the second stanza changes to the sounds he can hear and this continues until the end of the poem.

Everywhere he goes he sees people who are repressed and downtrodden; in the third stanza he hears the cry of a chimney sweep and the sigh of a soldier; in the final stanza, at night, at midnight, he hears the curse of *the youthful harlot* (very young prostitute) whose *curse* rings out in the night and *blasts* the *marriage-hearse*. We might note that there is no interaction between Blake and the sights and sounds he sees; the only interaction that there is evidence of is the *new-born infant* in the final stanza – the product of a sexual act – but the baby cries and is born into a world of misery and degradation. Nowhere in the poem do we meet a complete human being: we see their marks and hear them, but there is no encounter with any complete human being, suggesting at once their isolation, but also their lack of completeness and community in this horrifying city.

In the first stanza Blake uses simple repetition of the word *chartered* and *marks* (although with a slightly different meaning). The oppression he sees is all-consuming – he sees it in every face he meets. Note the last line which uses parallelism of sound:

Marks of weakness, marks of woe.

The word *mark* is repeated and is then followed by two words which alliterate. This combination of the letter *m* and *w* is very soft and gentle and creates a sense of overwhelming sadness. Note how *mark* starts as a verb in a very innocuous sense and then becomes a repeated noun, suggesting that there is an indelible mark on all the citizens of London.

The second stanza picks up the word *every* and repeats it five times to suggest the situation he is describing is all–encompassing. Again the final line is significant. The manacles that imprison people are *mind-forged* – they are forged, made in the mind. Is Blake suggesting that the people of London are not even aware of their own oppression? Is it something in their mentality, their minds, which prevents them from protesting? Do they have too much faith in their own rulers? Do they not question the system? Note too how Blake delays the verb of the second stanza – *I hear* – until the very last two words of the stanza. Blake's use of repetition in the first two stanzas has another purpose: his language becomes as restricted and limited as the lives of the people he describes. The word *ban* often stirs some debate: you may read elsewhere that it is a reference to the marriage banns – the announcements of a couple's intention to marry. This ties in with the final stanza, but, according to the Oxford English Dictionary, marriage banns have never been spelt with a single *n*. Isn't it more likely that Blake means prohibitions, banning something? Such as public meetings to protest about the condition of the country?

The third stanza continues with the sounds of London: the cry of the chimney sweep and the sigh of the soldier. Why is the church *black'ning*? Some readers suggest that it is a result of pollution caused by industry, but it could be a comment on the moral corruption of the church – it is evil. Why? I think Blake would suggest it is hypocritical: it is appalled by the cry of the chimney sweep, but does nothing to stop slavery and parents selling their children. The Church preaches a message of love, but does nothing practical to help the poor. The sibilance in lines 11 and 12 suggest the agony of the soldier. It is an astonishing image – sighs do not run in blood. But the soldier is badly wounded or dying – and he seems to be defending the palace or is at least in the pay of the place where the royal family live. Blake uses synecdoche to great effect in this stanza with his use of the words *church* and *palace*: its use here is partly to protect Blake in the repressive society he lived in, but it also serves to distance the establishment and the royal family even further from their subjects.

The worst horrors are saved until the fourth stanza and Blake signals this by stating – *but most* – and what he hears most of all is the curse of the youthful harlot. You can sometimes read that this is a curse in the sense of a bad spell, but it might just as well be a shouted swear word (*curse* had that meaning too). Who she is cursing is unclear, but the curse *blasts the new-born infant's tear*. Perhaps this is an unwanted baby, another mouth to feed, its father one of her clients? The baby is crying and in the final cryptic, oxymoronic line, her curse *blights with plagues the marriage hearse.*

The phrase *marriage hearse* is an oxymoron because we normally associate marriage with new life and happiness, whereas we associate hearses with funerals and sadness, so to put the two ideas together is striking and original. Does Blake mean that some marriages are like death? Or that marriage is the death of love? Is marriage something that the youthful harlot will never know? Or is it the marriage of one of her clients? Why do married men visit prostitutes? Some readers even suggest that the curse of the harlot is some sort of sexually transmitted sexual disease which the harlot has given to her client who has then passed it on to his wife – this reading might be supported by the word *plagues*. But *plagues* can be a metaphor too – whatever interpretation you choose, it is wise not to be too dogmatic – the beauty and brilliance of Blake is that he is able to suggest all the above possibilities – and even more.

What is certain is that there is something very wrong with marriage in this final stanza and that the curse of the harlot is frightening and chilling: note Blake's use of harsh plosive consonants in *blasts, blights and plagues* – this is almost onomatopoeic in its presentation of a diseased, corrupt society and Blake's angry reaction to it. We have already mentioned the oxymoron with which the poem ends, but Blake in the third stanza had already juxtaposed things which are not normally associated with each other: the cry of the chimney sweep with the church, and the sigh of the soldier with the palace walls – both these images in a way are oxymoronic. Think back to our comments on 'The Sick Rose' in the introduction – this is a profound and moving criticism of Blake's society.

Finally, Blake's use of the ballad form is important. The ballad form is associated with the oral tradition and with anonymity – it is a more democratic form than the sonnet. However, traditional ballads have a strong narrative drive which this poem lacks. So we can say that Blake takes a form that is popular and egalitarian, and then turns its narrative conventions upside down by writing a poem that is descriptive.

The Final Unpublished Stanza

This is the stanza that was found in Blake's notebooks when he died and which some editions of his complete works publish. As you read it, think about why Blake did not publish this stanza during his lifetime:

Remove away that blackening church;

Remove away that marriage hearse;

Remove away that man of blood –

You'll quite remove the ancient curse!

This makes explicit what is implied in the poem: Blake is calling for a revolution which will *remove* the church and the monarchy: *man of blood* is a phrase famously used by Oliver Cromwell to describe Charles I, the English king who was executed after losing the English Civil War. One can only guess why Blake did not include this stanza, but we can speculate that in 1794 it was too dangerous and that Blake might have got in trouble with the authorities for publishing such a call. Artistically the stanza has its limitations: *remove away* is tautological and, because it makes completely clear Blake's attitude to the things described in the poem as we read it today, one can argue that takes away the cryptic, mysterious quality of Blake's poem as it first appeared. This cryptic nature of the poem encourages us to think and analyze what Blake is saying and thus we are encouraged by the poem to break out of our own *mind-forged manacles*, to expand our minds in order to realize the full impact, the complete implications of what Blake's view of London is. London needs to be changed urgently and by a revolution.

Conflict and Power

The clear holders of power in this poem are the monarchy, the Church and the State. They use their power to oppress the population of London. There are clear hints of conflict in the poem – the chimney sweeper's cry, the soldier's sigh, the curse of the harlot – but the inhabitants of London are rendered essentially powerless by their "mind-forged manacles". They suffer from what Karl Marx was to call "false consciousness" – they are oppressed but are unaware of their oppression. In a sense, there is conflict between the poet and his fellow citizens: he sees their "marks of weakness", he hears the sounds of sadness and suffering, but he does so alone. His fellow citizens are trapped in their "mind-forged manacles". The final unpublished stanza, with its unambiguous call to revolution, indicates the power that the masses have – if they choose to use it.

A Romantic Poem?

Three key features of 'London' make it a typical Romantic poem. Blake's political stance – radical, revolutionary and anti-authoritarian – tie in perfectly with the Romantic desire for political change and reform. His hostile attitude to the Church, the State and the monarchy. In the poem the speaker is identified as different from his fellow citizens – he sees and hears things that they ignore: this marks the Romantic poet as a visionary, a seer with insights which he must communicate to his fellow citizens through his art. Finally, Blake's choice of the ballad stanza – a form originally associated with anonymous medieval writing – also demonstrates Blake's egalitarian credentials. Yet Blake puts the ballad form to a new use: traditionally ballads were a narrative form – poems that told stories – but Blake presents a series of insights into the inequalities of the London of his day.

Why?

This very famous poem is remarkable.

- It is a political poem of protest against the authorities.

- This sense of protest makes it an angry and bitter poem.

- It is typically Romantic in its concern for freedom and equality, and its anti-authoritarian stance.

- Blake speaks up for the marginalized in his society.

- It uses the ballad form in a revolutionary way.

- It is remarkable for its compression of language. Blake manages to pack so much meaning into so few words.

- Its use of simple repetition, sound effects and oxymoronic imagery make it memorable and striking.

'The Prelude' (stealing the boat) – William Wordsworth

Context

William Wordsworth was born in 1770 in Cockermouth on the edge of the English Lake District. He had a life-long fascination with nature and it is from the natural world that he took much of his inspiration. He died in 1850, having been made Poet Laureate in 1843. Wordsworth began to write *The Prelude* in 1798 and kept working on it and revising it until his death. It was not published until 1850, three months after his death. He published many poems during his own lifetime, but many readers feel that *The Prelude* is his finest work.

This extract is from *The Prelude*, a long autobiographical poem first finished in 1805. It is subtitled *The Growth of the Poet's Mind* – and Wordsworth tells the story of his life, but with the intention of showing his psychological development and also how he came to be a poet. Central to his development, he claims, was the influence of nature: Wordsworth grew up in the English Lake District – a national park and an area of outstanding natural beauty even today. It is not just that Wordsworth liked the beauty of nature – we perhaps all do that because we associate it with peace, away from the hustle and bustle of urban or suburban life; he also believed that nature had a moral influence on him and had made him a better human being. He is at pains throughout *The Prelude* to try and prove this connection – that his experiences in the natural world made him a better person and a poet. You may elsewhere read references to Wordsworth's pantheism. Pantheists worship nature and feel that if there is a God then that God exists in every living thing, every part of the natural world: God is a spirit of the universe which exists in a rock or a daffodil as much as it does in a human being.

her – Nature.

elfin pinnace – a pinnace is a small boat; elfin means small and charming.

covert – secret.

bark – boat.

Who? The poet narrates in the past tense an incident from his childhood.

When? 1805. Wordsworth was a child in the late 18th century, but is recollecting this experience as an adult.

Where? On a lake in the English Lake District, generally thought to be Ullswater.

What? Wordsworth steals a boat and goes for a row on the lake. He explores the ramifications of this incident on his conscience.

Commentary

This extract is written in blank verse. It narrates an incident. This extract comes from Book II of *The Prelude* which is entitled *Childhood and School-Time*. The opening sentence clearly shows the influence of Nature on the young Wordsworth:

One summer evening (led by her) I found

A little boat tied to a willow tree.

We know that *her* refers to nature from the preceding lines. The poet proceeds to unchain the boat and take it for an illicit row on the lake. In effect, Wordsworth is stealing the boat: he describes it as *an act of stealth* (he doesn't want to get caught) and uses an oxymoron - *troubled pleasure* – to show us that he has mixed feelings about what he is doing: he knows it is wrong. Lines 8–11 use a variety of sound effects and very positive vocabulary to present the initial experience of this escapade. He says the boat left behind her

still, on either side,

Small circles glittering idly in the moon,

Until they melted all into one track

Of sparkling light.

Listen to those lines: Wordsworth uses no figurative language, but there is a preponderance of *s*, *l* and *m* sounds which give a gentle, restful feeling which reinforces the meanings of the words. The lines are given more aural coherence by assonance: *side/idly/light* and by consonance - *track/sparkling*. Wordsworth has decided to row across the lake and has picked out a craggy ridge as his landmark towards which he is heading.

This positive tone and atmosphere continues up to line 20. The boat is an *elfin pinnace* – playful, mischievous (like an elf) – and the boat moves through the water *like a swan* – a beautiful, majestic bird.

And then the whole tone changes. By a trick of perspective, as Wordsworth rows across the lake, a huge peak comes into view. When you row, you face the direction you started from and the further Wordsworth rows from the shore of the lake, the mountains behind his starting point start to appear. Look at how the poet describes it and his response to it:

a huge peak, black and huge,

As if with voluntary power instinct,

Upreared its head. I struck and struck again,

And growing still in stature the grim shape

Towered up between me and the stars, and still,

For so it seemed, with purpose of its own

And measured motion like a living thing,

Strode after me.

Like nature, like the boat, the peak is personified and takes on a life of its own, but note also the way a sense of panic in the poet is created by simple repetition of *huge* and *struck*; these lines are full of sibilance too – which creates a sinister, hissing sound. Wordsworth's reaction is one of guilt and shame:

With trembling oars I turned,

And through the silent water stole my way.

He puts the boat back where he found it and then finds he is haunted by this experience for many days afterwards. He does not fully understand what has happened to him:

my brain

Worked with a dim and undetermined sense

Of unknown modes of being.

He is also depressed by the experience:

o'er my thoughts

There hung a darkness, call it solitude

Or blank desertion.

He cannot take his customary pleasure in nature – *No familiar shapes remained* – and his every waking thought and even his sleep is disturbed by

huge and mighty forms that do not live

Like living men, moved slowly through the mind

By day, and were a trouble to my dreams.

How are we to interpret this poem? If some of the language towards the end of the extract seems a little vague, it is because Wordsworth himself – as a small boy – is struggling to make sense of what happened to him.

What is certain is that this experience is a formative one and leads to an epiphany: the poet is made to feel guilty for taking the boat and in that sense it is an important part of Wordsworth's intention – to show that we can learn morality from nature – not just from books or other people. And so nature is presented as beautiful and inspiring, but also frightening if you do something wrong or immoral. The huge and mighty forms that haunt the young boy's mind in the days that follow the incident seem to suggest that there is a divinity in nature, that the natural world (as Wordsworth sees it) is an expression of the existence of God and one which punishes us when we commit immoral acts – like stealing someone else's boat.

We can also see this extract as charting the passage from innocence to experience, from childhood to adulthood. In the first part of the extract Wordsworth is totally in control – of the boat, the situation and his emotions. What he is doing may be wrong but it is clearly enjoyable for a brief period: this can be seen as showing how attractive it is to sin – we are tempted to do wrong because some sins are very attractive and pleasurable. But the sudden appearance of the mountain changes everything and shows the young poet that he is not in control: there is a higher power that watches over us. In simpler terms we might say that the mountain symbolizes his guilty conscience.

Conflict and Power

This extract is remarkable for the power that Nature has over the young Wordsworth. Nature's influence makes him feel guilt for his casual theft of the boat and exerts a moral influence on him lasting for a long time after the incident. The long poem – *The Prelude* (from which this is an extract) – is full of examples of nature's influence on Wordsworth's spiritual and moral development, demonstrating Wordsworth's Pantheism. There is conflict in the poem too: again the conflict centres around the theft of the boat, and it really involves the internal conflict and guilt that Wordsworth feels and which is heightened by Nature and the looming crag that seems to rise up and overpower him. Wordsworth's personification, his animation of Nature greatly aids the impression on the reader.

A Romantic Poem?

This extract is typically Romantic as is the whole of *The Prelude*. The very act of writing a long autobiographical poem about himself suggests that Wordsworth considers himself an exceptional individual with important truths to convey through his poetry. The supreme importance given to nature – in this passage and elsewhere in *The Prelude* – also marks it out as typically romantic, as does Wordsworth's pantheistic notion that Nature is a living force that can inculcate morality.

Why?

This very famous extract:

- shows nature as a moral and spiritual guide.

- explores the psychology of a young boy and his intense feelings of guilt.

- the importance it attaches to Nature make it a typically Romantic poem.

- explores the attractiveness of wrong-doing, but also the effects of a guilty conscience.

- demonstrates a deep love of and respect for nature.

- focuses very closely on the individual and his relationship with nature.

'My Last Duchess' – Robert Browning

Context

Robert Browning was born in 1812 and became one of the most famous English poets of the Victorian era. He was married to Elizabeth Barrett Browning who was a semi-invalid with an over-protective father. The couple were married in secret and then went to live in Italy. Browning's best work is often set in the past and he was a master of the dramatic monologue, in which the imagined speaker of the poem reveals their innermost thoughts and feelings, often going on to uncover uncomfortable truths about themselves.

This poem is based on real historical events. Duke Alfonso II of Modena and Ferrara (1559 – 1597) married Lucrezia de Doctors and she died four years after the wedding in mysterious circumstances. This is the starting point for Browning's poem. Victorian Britain was rather obsessed with the Italian Renaissance. Many of Browning's monologues are set in Renaissance Italy. The Renaissance, around the period 1450 – 1650, was a cultural and intellectual movement which happened all across Western Europe and it involved the rediscovery of many of the skills that had been forgotten or ignored since the fall of the Roman Empire, especially in painting, art and sculpture. We can understand why the Renaissance began in Italy and the Italians felt themselves to be the heirs of the ancient Romans. In Italy the ruins and ancient buildings were a constant visual reminder of the arts of Rome. The artistic achievement of the Renaissance was helped by a system of patronage: wealthy dukes, merchants and princes commissioned great artists to create paintings and sculptures, just as in the poem the Duke of Ferrara has commissioned Fra Pandolf to paint the portrait of his first wife and Claus of Innsbruck has sculpted Neptune taming a sea-horse.

But the Renaissance, especially in Italy, had a sinister side to it. Many of the wealthy and powerful patrons of art were just as capable of paying to have an enemy assassinated or poisoned because their power and wealth they had allowed them to do so. What seems to have fascinated the Victorians was the co-existence in the Italian renaissance of art works of stunning beauty alongside moral and political corruption. As Victorian Britons they hoped to emulate the cultural achievements, but looked down upon (even as they were fascinated by) the moral corruption.

Fra Pandolf – an imaginary painter who supposedly painted the portrait of the Duchess.

a day – for many days.

countenance – face.

durst – dared.

mantle – a cloak.

favour – a thing (a jewelled brooch perhaps or a flower) worn as a token of love or affection.

officious – too forward in offering unwelcome or unwanted services.

nine-hundred-years-old name – this simply means that the title the Duke of Ferrara was first created nine-hundred years before the poem is set.

forsooth – truly.

the Count, your master – this phrase is important because it makes clear that the speaker of the poem is talking to a servant of the Count, who is visiting (it later becomes clear) to discuss the marriage of his daughter to the narrator.

munificence – generosity.

nay – no.

Neptune – the God of the Sea.

Claus of Innsbruck – an imaginary sculptor who has sculpted the statue of Neptune for the Duke.

Who? The Duke of Ferrara talks to the representative of an unnamed count who is there to arrange for his daughter to marry the Duke – she will be his next duchess. The poem is written in the present tense.

When? In the 16th century, in the Duke's palace. This is very important because Browning and his fellow Victorians were fascinated by the Italian Renaissance period.

Where? In Ferrara in northern Italy.

What? The speaker tells the story of his first marriage by reference to a portrait of his first wife which hangs on the wall.

Commentary

'My Last Duchess' by Robert Browning is a very famous and much-anthologized poem. It is a dramatic monologue – that is to say the poet adopts the voice of someone else and speaks throughout as that person. It was first published in 1842 and is one of many dramatic monologues that Browning wrote.

The speaker in the poem is the Duke of Ferrara, an Italian nobleman from the 16th century – we are told this from the note at the beginning. This immediately tells us the location of the poem (Italy) and the social background of the speaker – he is a powerful and wealthy aristocrat.

As the poem develops we come to understand that the Duke (pictured here) is talking to a representative of the family of his fiancée, his future wife, and that they are talking in the Duke of Ferrara's palace. We can be even more precise and say that for most of the poem they are standing in front of a portrait of the Duke's former wife (now dead). The Duke talks about his dead wife and, in doing so, reveals a great deal abut his character, the sort of man he is. We also learn the terrible fate of his first wife.

The opening sentence refers the reader to a painting hanging on the wall. The painting is so good that his previous wife is

Looking as if she were alive.

Browning establishes that the painter was skilled and produced a *wonder* – a masterpiece. The painter fussed over the portrait and over the duchess – *his hands worked busily a day.* In line 5 we realize for the first time that the duke is speaking not to the readers as such, but someone else; he invites him to sit and look at the portrait of his dead wife. He says he mentioned Fra Pandolf *by design* – perhaps to imply that he was an exceptionally well-known and highly sought-after painter (but remember that he is has been made up by Browning). The fact that the Duke could pay for his services shows his rich he is.

The long sentence that begins on line 5 may be a little hard to follow. Note that in lines 9-10 the duke reveals that the painting is normally concealed by a curtain which only he is allowed to open; this suggests, perhaps, a man who is used to being obeyed, even in petty things like a curtain covering a painting. When people like the person he is talking to – *strangers like you* – see the painting, the duke says, they are always moved to ask him (he's always there because he controls the curtain!) what caused the *depth and passion* in the look on the duchess's face. You might note the phrase *its pictured countenance* – I know he is talking about a painted image, but it may strike you as unusual that he doesn't use the word *her* when talking about his dead wife. This one word suggests that he treated her like an object in life and, now that her portrait is on his wall, she is still an object – only now he can exert complete control over her. We might also note that the visitor hasn't asked about the *earnest glance* in the duchess's face – perhaps only the duke sees it. He seems to like the painting of her very much indeed and we will return to this idea later in this commentary.

The duke continues by saying that his visitor is not the first person to ask him why she looked so passionate in the portrait. The duke states

.... Sir, 'twas not

Her husband's presence only, called that spot

Of joy into the Duchess' cheek.

Her husband's presence – are we to assume that he was there in the room all the time while she had her portrait completed? I think we are – it fits with what we are starting to find out about his character. The duke seems to have been jealous when other men paid any attention to his wife – something she appears to have enjoyed since it brings *a spot of joy* to her face. He seems to have seen Fra Pandolf as some sort of rival and repeats things that the painter said to his wife in lines 16 – 19. You may feel that the duke really suspected that Fra Pandolf was his wife's secret lover or you may feel that the duke thought she was a little too easily impressed by male attention.

The duke then expands on his wife's faults. She was *too soon made glad*; she was *too easily impressed*; she could not discriminate –

...she liked whate'er

She looked on and her looks went everywhere.

She looked on everything with the same undiscriminating affection.

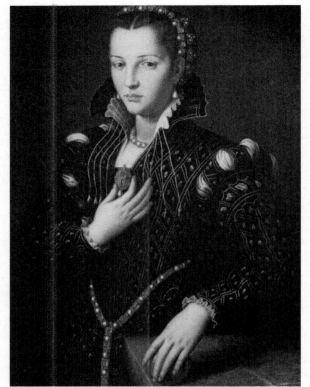

My favour at her breast — some precious brooch pinned on her breast and given her by the duke was given the same importance as the sunset or some cherries brought to her by a servant or riding a white mule along the terrace of the palace. You might feel that riding a white mule is a slightly eccentric thing to do — but she is the wife of a wealthy and very powerful man and she can do what she likes, whatever takes her fancy. Above is a picture believed to be of the Duchess that the poem is based upon.

Line 33 reveals the duke's arrogance about his title and position. He talks about his nine-hundred-years-old name and clearly feels that his position and his title as Duke of Ferrara should have been given more respect by his wife. Note that he calls his name *My gift* – as though she should have been grateful that he married her.

In line 34 he starts to suggest that his attitude to all this was casual and relaxed. He calls her behaviour *trifling* and says he would not *stoop* to blame her. *Stoop* is an important word because it reminds us of his high social status and makes it clear that he regarded his wife as beneath him and inferior to him: it is a word that he repeats in the next few lines. And so it was that, even though his wife's behaviour disgusted him, he never said a word.

Browning allows the duke to say he is not good at speaking and so may not have been able to explain his misgivings to his wife – but this is sheer nonsense: every line of this poem shows that the duke (as Browning has created him) is a clever manipulator of words. He says that she might have argued with him: *plainly set her wits* against his; and that even if he could have explained, it would have been degrading for him to have done so

E'en then would be some stooping, and I choose

Never to stoop.

Once again we are reminded of his arrogance and superciliousness. It is interesting that he could not speak to his wife, but he takes 56 lines of the poem to talk to his visitor. She remained friendly to him – she smiled when she passed him, but she smiled at everyone and his sense of his own importance cannot allow that. And then we come to the heart, perhaps, of the poem

... I gave commands;

Then all smiles stopped together.

The duke gave some orders and had his wife murdered. This is quite clear. Browning said of the poem in an interview:

I meant that the commands were that she should be put to death....Or he might have had her shut up in a convent.

Now look back at line 19. It refers to the painter saying that he can never hope to reproduce in paint *the flush that dies along her throat* – that fades along her throat, but now we have read more of the poem and we know what the duke did to his wife, it is clear that Browning is preparing us verbally for the truth. Did she have her throat slashed? Or was she strangled? Either could be true. The flush in line 19 is the way that the Duchess blushed when she was flirting, perhaps, but the fact that Browning uses the verb 'dies' instead of 'fade' is a way of verbally prefiguring her fate. And his final sentence about his wife also suggests that she was murdered: *there she stands/ As if alive.*

In line 47 he invites his visitor to stand and go downstairs with him to meet the company – the group of people who are waiting for them down below. Line 49 reveals that he has been talking to a servant of an unnamed Count (*your master*) whose *known munificence* means that he (the duke) expects a very large dowry. Having mentioned the dowry, the duke asserts that he doesn't really care about money – he is only interested in the count's daughter.

As they go down the stairs the duke points out a bronze statue, another of his pieces of art, sculpted by Claus of Innsbruck for him. The statue's subject matter is important: it shows the god of the sea, Neptune, taming a sea-horse. This demonstrates the relationship that the duke had with his first wife (he tamed her), with his servants and with his future wife – the daughter of the Count. Like Neptune ruling the sea, the duke likes to have power over people and beautiful objects like the painting of his wife and this statue. It is significant that the final word of this poem is *me* – because the duke's self-centredness has slowly been revealed the more we have read.

Browning writes in rhyming couplets of ten syllables, but his use of enjambment means that, because the lines are very rarely end-stopped, the poem drives onwards, just as the duke almost compulsively reveals what has happened to his wife. The enjambment also prevents the rhyming couplets from becoming too monotonous and make them sound more like real speech. The duke's hesitations and frequent interjections make him appear reasonable, although he is talking about the murder of his first wife. He has a very casual attitude to it all: he acquired a wife; she did not behave as he liked; he disposed of her. The naturalness of the sound of his speech, its casual, relaxed tone suggests that he does not see anything wrong in what he has done and expects his listener to find it normal too.

Although he claims he is not skilled in speaking, Browning ensures that the Duke gradually reveals the truth about what happened to his wife and the truth about his own character: he is possessive, jealous and likes the idea of controlling people. He is proud and arrogant about his aristocratic title and his family's history. He seems to prefer the painting of his dead wife to her living reality: he can control the painting, but he could not control his first wife. The poem ends on an note of dread – dread on behalf of his second wife who does not know what lies in store for her. He also seems to treat his wives like objects: objects are much easier to control than living human beings.

He seems more interested in being seen as a man of great taste than as a good husband. He draws the servant's attention to the painting and to the sculpture at the end. These objects are meant to demonstrate his taste and his wealth – he is connected to the great artists of his day. But his taste is limited to things he can control and totally possess – for example, he does not seem to be aware of the irony in the sculpture of Neptune and the fact that it might symbolize his relationships with other people, especially women.

Conflict and Power

The Duke of Ferrara exercises complete power in his palace and its grounds. His power is based on his aristocratic positon – his "nine hundred year old name", his money, and his possessive and jealous personality. There is a paradox here: despite all his money and power, he could not control the behaviour of his wife and – "I gave commands" – he gets rid of his troublesome wife. Now she exists as a painting, covered by curtains which only he can use, so he now has a measure of control over her. His power is also shown by the quick way in which his commands were acted upon and also by his collection of expensive and exquisite works of art. Because this is a dramatic monologue, Browning presents the Duke without comment – in marked contrast to the three preceding Romantic poems where the reader is left in no doubt about the poet's own views. With this poem Browning presents the Duke and allows the reader to make up their own mind about him.

Why?

This casual-sounding but deeply sinister poem

- shows the pride and arrogance of the aristocracy.

- is a portrait of the psychology of a murderer.

- shows that money and status and power can corrupt.

- shows the domination of men over women.

- raises questions about the relationship between art and life.

- is superbly written by Browning so that the reader must read between the lines as the terrible truth dawns upon us.

'The Charge of the Light Brigade' – Alfred, Lord Tennyson

Context

Alfred Tennyson was born in 1809 and died in 1892. His early work received a mixed reaction, but his *Poems* published in 1842 established him as the leading poet of his day. In 1850 he was made Poet Laureate and was given a peerage in 1884. This poem is not especially typical of his work. It was published in 1855 in a collection called *Maud* and was written in response to a British military disaster during the Battle of Balaklava in October 1854. It is said that Tennyson read the report of the disaster in *The Times* and was moved to write the poem.

The Crimean War was fought largely in the Crimean Peninsula – then part of the Russian Empire and was until recently part of the Ukraine before the Crimean Peninsula was annexed by Russia in 2014. Britain and its allies – France and the Ottoman Empire – were fighting Russia over who would control the Dardenelles – the narrow strip of sea in Turkey that connects the Aegean Sea to the Black Sea. It was important for British sea-routes and trade that Russia did not control the Dardenelles, but it was important for Russia as it gave her access to the Mediterranean.

This is the report from *The Times* that Tennyson read:

At ten past eleven our Light Cavalry Brigade rushed to the front....The whole brigade scarcely made one effective regiment, according to the numbers of continental armies; and yet it was more than we could spare. As they passed towards the front, the Russians opened on them from the guns in the redoubts on the right, with volleys of musketry and rifles.

They swept proudly past, glittering in the morning sun in all the pride and splendour of war. We could hardly believe the evidence of our senses! Surely that handful of men were not going to charge an army in position? Alas! it was too true – their desperate valour knew no bounds, and far indeed was it removed from its so called better part – discretion. They advanced in two lines, quickening their pace as they closed towards the enemy. A more fearful spectacle was never witnessed than by those who, without the power to aid, beheld their heroic countrymen rushing to the arms of death. At the distance of 1200 yards the whole line of the enemy belched forth, from thirty iron mouths, a flood of smoke and flame, through which hissed the deadly balls. Their flight was marked by instant gaps in our ranks, by dead men and horses, by steeds flying wounded or riderless across the plain. The first line was broken – it was joined by the second, they never halted or checked their speed an instant. With diminished ranks, thinned by those thirty guns, which the Russians had laid with the most deadly accuracy, with a halo of flashing steel above their heads, and with a cheer which was many a noble fellow's death cry, they flew into the smoke of the batteries; but ere they were lost from view, the plain was strewed with their bodies and with the carcasses of horses. They were exposed to an oblique fire from the batteries on the hills on both sides, as well as to a direct fire of musketry.

Through the clouds of smoke we could see their sabres flashing as they rode up to the guns and dashed between them, cutting down the gunners as they stood. The blaze of their steel, as an officer standing near me said, was 'like the turn of a shoal of mackerel'. We saw them riding through the guns, as I have said; to our delight we saw them returning, after breaking through a column of Russian infantry, and scattering them like chaff, when the flank fire of the battery on the hill swept them down, scattered and broken as they were. Wounded men and dismounted troopers flying towards us told the sad tale – demigods could not have done what they had failed to do.

At the very moment when they were about to retreat, an enormous mass of lancers was hurled upon their flank…With courage too great almost for credence, they were breaking their way through the columns which enveloped them, when there took place an act of atrocity without parallel in the modern warfare of civilized nations. The Russian gunners, when the storm of cavalry passed, returned to their guns. They saw their own cavalry mingled with the troopers who had just ridden over them, and to the eternal disgrace of the Russian name the miscreants poured a murderous volley of grape and canister on the mass of struggling men and horses, mingling friend and foe in one common ruin…At twenty five to twelve not a British soldier, except the dead and dying, was left in front of these bloody Muscovite guns.

And this is what *The Times* editorial said about the disaster:

Causeless and fruitless, it stands by itself as a grand heroic deed, surpassing even that spectacle of a shipwrecked regiment, setting down into the waves, each man still in his rank. The British soldier will do his duty, even to certain death, and is not paralyzed by feeling that he is the victim of **some hideous blunder.** [My emboldening.]

Why have I bothered to reprint this article? I think it is important for you to see the inspiration that Tennyson used. He had not been to the Crimea; he had never been on a battlefield; his only source was this article. *Some hideous blunder* is directly reflected in line 12 of the poem. Equally the reporter's assertion that the British soldier will *do his duty, even to certain death is* the main theme of the poem. The Light Brigade began the charge with 607 men; only 302 returned. I think *The Times* report is interesting – not simply because it is a first-hand account by a journalist who witnessed the event. The editorial admits there was *some hideous blunder*, but the overwhelming tone of the report and the editorial is admiration for the courage of the men who obeyed such a senseless order. We can see in Tennyson's poem a similar balance: he does admit it was a terrible mistake, but his emphasis is on the heroism of the men who simply obeyed their orders.

In reality, the incident was a complete failure and a pointless loss of life – it was a military disaster. However, it has become famous, partly through Tennyson's poem, but also because it moved other artists to produce work based on the incident. Perhaps it appealed to something that the public wanted to believe was part of being British – unflinching courage against the odds. Over the course of time, Tennyson's poem has lost some of its popularity perhaps because our attitudes to war have changed and we are more likely to question the justness of any war and the human cost of blindly following orders. In Tennyson's defence, one might say that as Poet Laureate it was his task to reflect the national mood at the time and it is certainly true that the men who charged on that day did display great courage.

league – three miles

Valley of Death – an allusion to Psalm 23 in the Bible and to a novel called *Pilgrim's Progress* by John Bunyan. In both texts faith in God encourages people to be brave in dangerous places.

Light Brigade – at school I was confused about this title. It means that the brigade were on horseback but were lightly armed – they only carried swords. And, yes – there was a Heavy Brigade who moved more slowly because they carried more weaponry.

sabres – the specific type of sword carried by the soldiers.

Cossack – an ethnic group from south-eastern Russia, famed for their fighting skills and bravery.

sunder'd – broken apart

Back from the mouth of Hell – anthropologists have noted that in cultures all over the world there are stories about brave men who visit hell or the underworld or the world of the dead and return alive. For example, in Greek mythology Hercules visits the underworld, but returns unscathed, adding to his heroic qualities. Tennyson is deliberately adding the members of the Light Brigade to this long and brave tradition.

Who? Tennyson writes about the cavalrymen of the Light Brigade; the enemy is present in the poem, as is the person who gave the order to charge the Russian guns; the reader is addressed directly in the final stanza.

When? October 25th, 1854, although Tennyson wrote the poem a few days later having read the report in *The Times*.

Where? Outside the Russian town of Balaklava in the Crimean Peninsula.

What? Tennyson describes the charge of the cavalry and what happened to them.

Commentary

This very famous poem relies a great deal on repetition throughout its length. Tennyson also uses alliteration in many lines and, if you read it aloud, the rhythm of the poem seems to imitate the motion of the horses galloping forward. It is these features, I would suggest, which make the poem so memorable.

The opening stanza highlights the order the brigade was given in lines 5 and 6. The opening phrase is repeated three times; *Valley of Death* is repeated twice as is *the six hundred* – giving these phrases prominence and emphasizing that they are going to die and their relatively small numbers. The phrase *Valley of Death* would have been very evocative to a Christian audience because it comes from such a well-known psalm.

The second stanza is directly related to the report in *The Times*. Line 9 repeats line 5. Line 12 picks up the word used by the journalist, but makes the order anonymous – *Someone had blunder'd*. It is not part of Tennyson's aim to apportion blame for the order, but to praise the men who followed it. And it is important, in the poem, that the soldiers knew it was a blunder yet still went ahead and charged: it shows their blind obedience to orders and their bravery. Lines 13 to 15 use repetition but also heap praise on their unquestioning obedience of the order, despite having a clear understanding that it would lead to death. The alliteration in line 15 – *do and die* – draws attention their clear courage and willingness to die.

In stanza three Tennyson makes us aware of the enemy again, through simple repetition which here gives us a real sense of the situation into which they rode, facing cannon fire from three sides. Note the onomatopoeia of *thunder'd* and the alliteration in line 22. In lines 24 and 25 Tennyson uses synonyms for the Valley of Death – *the jaws of Death* and *the mouth of Hell*. Although he concentrates on their bravery, line 23 also mentions their skill. They rode *well* and *boldly*, despite the terrible situation they were in.

Stanza four describes what happened when the cavalry reached the Russian positions. Tennyson uses vivid verbs – *flash'd, charging, plunged* – to give us an impression of close quarter fighting. *Charging an army* reminds us of the impossible odds they faced, while *All the world wonder'd* might mean that the world looks on amazed at their courage or astonished at the stupidity of the order – it probably means both! They have some limited success when in close contact with the enemy: the Russians *reel'd* and were *shatter'd and sunder'd*. Finally at the end of the stanza they turn to ride back to the British positions – those that are left. Note Tennyson's repeated use of the phrase *the six hundred*, except that it is now preceded by *not*.

The brigade ride back to their own positions in stanza five. Again Tennyson repeats several lines and phrases from earlier in the poem. The first three lines are identical to the start of stanza three with only one word being altered. He uses more alliteration in line 44 and pays tribute to the soldiers with the word *hero* and by pointing out that they had fought so well.

The sixth stanza is short and directly addressed to the reader. It begins with a question which stresses their glory (and not the idiocy of the order); the second line is an exclamation of admiration and is followed by a line we have seen before which suggests their charge will become famous all over the world. The final three lines are imperatives, orders to the readers – we are told to honour the Light Brigade because they were so noble.

How attitudes have changed since 1854! Today if so many British soldiers died in one engagement that lasted only half an hour, there would be a public outcry and calls for an enquiry – particularly if it emerged that they died because of an incompetent order or an order that was misinterpreted. But Tennyson is not interested in that side of this story and in the past such an inquiry is much less likely to have occurred. He wants to praise their unthinking bravery and willingness to die following orders. You may find it hard to agree with the attitudes in the poem, but there is no doubt that Tennyson uses all his poetic skills to create something memorable.

Conflict and Power

The questions of conflict and power are very ambivalent in this poem. Despite their appalling losses and the fact that this attack was a terrible failure, Tennyson manages to suggest the power of the Light Brigade's charge through his use of anapaests, coupled with the occasional trochee at the start of some lines. It is this which helps to make the charge sound heroic and brave. Of course, the Russian artillery are a major source of conflict and, throughout the charge, the Russians hold all the real power. More widely, the poem is about a wider conflict – the Crimean War. There is further conflict on the British side which Tennyson acknowledges: the ill-judged order for the Light Brigade to charge ("someone had blundered"), yet it is a tribute to the self-discipline of the Brigade that they obey the order. The power of discipline in the British Army is a quality which Tennyson's poem recognizes and celebrates, despite the disastrous result. Yet the real power in the poem is that of the Russian cannon which caused such heavy losses on the Light Brigade. The ultimate conflict in the poem is the unwavering courage of the members of the Light Brigade who obeyed without question an order which sent many of them to certain death and whether it was right for them to do so. I think a modern reader might feel some conflict, because Tennyson does glamourize war and its participants and our modern attitude to war is very diffferent

Why?

This very well-known and famous poem

- gives a vivid impression of the speed of the charge and the atmosphere of battle.

- glorifies the courage and heroism of the men who followed orders and made the charge.

- tells us to remember the dead and their noble deeds.

- is unashamedly patriotic and celebratory of the courage shown by the soldiers.

'Exposure' – Wilfred Owen

Context

 Wilfred Owen (1893 – 1918) is widely regarded as the leading British poet of the First World War. He died in action on November 4th 1918 – just seven days before the war finally came to an end. Owen was an officer and was awarded the Military Cross for leadership and bravery in October 1918. The shock of what he saw in the front-line moved him to produce a great many poems in a very short time – most of which were not published until after his death. He seems to have been particularly keen to ensure that the British public was told the horrific truth about the war. He developed his own use of half-rhyme which was to influence other poets for the whole of the 20th century. Owen famously wrote that his subject was not war, but the pity of war – a feeling that is especially apparent in this poem. "Above all I am not concerned with Poetry. My subject is War, and the pity of War. The Poetry is in the pity."

It is over a hundred years since the First World War began, and, because of the many commemorations, many readers will have a visual sense of what that war was like. In fact, it was a world war with fighting taking place on almost every continent, but the abiding memory of the war – a memory based on photos, documentaries and even poems like this one, is of the trench warfare on the Western Front in Belgium and France. There are clear reasons for this. The war waged in the trenches resulted in battles with enormous loss of life with very little ground gained: on the first day of the Battle of the Somme the British army suffered 70,000 casualties, 20,000 of whom were killed. I think the other reason the Western Front holds such an important place in our image of the First World War is the trenches themselves and trench life: hundreds of thousands of soldiers living very close to each other in holes in the ground and suffering terrible, barbaric conditions, plagued by rats, lice and the cold. So the futility and loss of life in the battles, as well as the appalling conditions make the war in the trenches especially memorable.

salient – a one-way trench dug out into No Man's Land to get closer to the enemy

melancholy – dejection, depression

glozed – decorated with

crickets – house crickets: insects which live near or behind old fireplaces and make a distinctive and rhythmic clicking sound

not loath – not unwilling

Who? Owen uses the third person plural – we – to speak on behalf of British soldiers fighting in trenches on the Western Front during the First World War.

When? Not specified, but in the depths of winter during the First World War.

Where? In the trenches of the Western Front. The First World War was a very static war: the trench systems of the Allies and of the Germans stretched from the coast of Belgium to the French border with Switzerland.

What? Owen describes a typical night and the following day in the trenches. The main enemy is not the Germans but the weather; the main feelings not fear or misgivings, but boredom and pointlessness. Owen reflects on why he and his colleagues are there and what they are fighting for.

Throughout the poem Owen speaks for all the soldiers on the Western Front by using "we" as they face an onslaught from – not the Germans – but the weather. The first stanza starts with a simple, straightforward statement: "Our brains ache in the merciless iced east winds that knive us" – the long vowels of the opening three words suggesting tiredness followed by sibilance and assonance on shorter vowels describing the wind, and ending with "knive us" which turns the wind into a stabbing knife, cutting into them. In the next line, although they cannot sleep, paradoxically it is because the night is silent and they anticipate an attack. They have confused memories of being in a salient and the only light comes from "low, drooping flares"; the sentries are "worried by silence… curious, nervous." But, as Owen tells us in the last line "nothing happens" – words which are repeated four times in the poem.

Owen establishes in the first verse the structure he will use for all eight stanzas of the poem: a five line stanza with the first line half-rhyming with the fourth, and the second and third line rhyming with each other. Half-rhyme (because it sounds wrong - to put it simply) is an apt choice for a poem in which the poet describes a situation where many things are wrong. Very often the rhyme words are trochees as well as being half-rhyme (*nervous/ knive us*) and this falling rhythm and the feminine endings to the lines intensify the sense of anti-climax and a poignant sort of futility. It also – along with the final shortened line produces a strange sense of apathy. The fifth and final line of each verse is much shorter than the others and acts as an anti-climax: again this is highly appropriate, because, despite all the nervous anticipation, this is a poem in which nothing happens. The fact that the fourth line rhymes with the first is important too: by the time the reader reaches the fourth line we are directed back to the first line by the half-rhyme. The stanza looks inward so to speak and this is appropriate in a poem which describes a stalemate and which is concerned largely with the inner thoughts and feelings of the soldiers.

The first word of the second stanza – "Watching" – suggests the soldiers' passivity: they have nothing to do except wait, but their senses are keenly attuned to their surroundings and the possibility of attack. They hear the "mad gusts tugging on the [barbed] wire" which only serves to remind them of the "twitching agonies" of men caught and dying on the wire. From the north "the flickering gunnery rumbles" – a striking image which combines an image of light with onomatopoeia and is given aural cohesion by the assonance in "gunnery rumbles", assonance which is continued in the next line with "dull rumour". The stanza ends with the poignant question: "What are we doing here?"

In the third stanza dawn comes but it brings no respite, no hope. The soldiers give the impression of being reduced to survival of the elements: "We only know war lasts, rain soaks, and clouds sag stormy" Owen then introduces a metaphor related to the war to describe the heavy rain clouds that are heading their way:

Dawn massing in the east her melancholy army

Attacks once more in ranks on shivering ranks of grey.

The German army wore grey uniforms which makes the personification even more apposite, but only rain faces the soldiers. And once again "Nothing happens."

The fourth stanza begins with a superbly written line, the sibilance of 's' giving an aural impression of the sound of gunfire. But it is not threatening and Owen remarks that the bullets are "less deadly than the air that shudders black with snow". The next line alliterates on 'f' to describe the gentle snowflakes and the caesuras and verbs – "flock, pause and renew" attempt to suggest the swirling, random movement of the snowflakes. The soldiers are reduced to passivity again – watching the snowflakes. "But still nothing happens".

The next stanza shows how exposed the British soldiers were to the elements: it's as if the snowflakes are deliberately seeking them out:

Pale flakes with lingering stealth come feeling for our faces.

And here the personification and the "stealth" make the snowflakes appear especially malevolent. The personification of the snowflakes and the phrase "come feeling for our faces" suggests a curiously evil intimacy. As the soldiers "cringe in holes" their minds reminisce about happier times – of "grassier ditches" and "blossoms trickling where the blackbird fusses". But the stanza ends on an ominous note as Owen asks "Is it that we are dying?" The uncertainty engendered by the question is deliberately unnerving.

The sixth stanza is a respite from the weather. "Slowly our ghosts drag home" and the soldiers think about their homes, but the thought brings little joy as the house belongs to the crickets and the mice:

The house is theirs;

Shutter and doors are closed: on us the doors are closed –

We turn back to our dying.

The seventh stanza appears to offer a justification for the war. If we follow the sense from the previous stanza:

We turn back to our dying.

Since we believe not otherwise can kind fires burn;

Nor ever suns smile true on child, or field, or fruit.

These lines imply that the soldiers are there to ensure that "kind fires can burn" and that because of their participation in the war suns will smile true on "child, or field, or fruit". Paradoxically their love is made afraid of "God's invincible spring" which suggests that they believe that God is on their side, Winter will be displaced by Spring and – ironically – the better weather will allow real fighting to begin – which is why they are afraid. But, conscious that they are defending a just cause, "we lie out here; therefore were born" – which suggests that what they are doing is both their destiny and their duty. However, Owen's faith in the Christian God is given a tentative rebuke when he writes "but love of God seems dying" – how could God allow such horrendous suffering on such a colossal scale?

But despite this stanza of justification, Owen in the final stanza returns to the grim reality of winter in the trenches:

Tonight, His frost will fasten on this mud and us,

Shrivelling many hands and puckering foreheads crisp.

"His frost" is God's frost; there seems little evidence of God's love for suffering humanity in this poem.And during the night some men will die of hypothermia, to be buried on the next day:

The burying party, picks and shovels in their shaking grasp,

Pause over half-known faces. All their eyes are ice.

But nothing happens.

Owen has succeeded in writing a poem which details in excruciating detail the desperate conditions endured in winter in the trenches, where the main enemy was not the German Army but the atrocious winter weather – men literally froze to death. He also conveys a sense of the sheer boredom of waiting for something, anything, to happen and questions repeatedly what the soldiers are doing there. He also includes two verses which allow the men to think about their homes and offers a justification for their being there – to allow kind fires to burn.

"Exposure" is not one of Owen's best-known poems, but perhaps it deserves to be: the use of half-rhyme, the stanza structure that turns in upon itself, and the truncated last line are wholly appropriate to the subject matter of the poem – the soldiers' doubts about why they are there and their doubt about God's role in their suffering. I find the last short line of each stanza especially effective since it leads nowhere – just as the men are going nowhere and seem to have lost all purpose.

Conflict and Power

The central conflict in 'Exposure' is between the atrocious weather conditions and the British soldiers defenceless against the rain, the snow and the frost. In the final verse some men have frozen to death overnight. The war is irrelevant in this poem. Another source of conflict is the sheer boredom the soldiers experience, waiting for something to happen and the doubts they have about why they are there – doing nothing except battling the atrocious weather conditions. Stanza six shows the conflict between the men's memories of home and their current experiences. While stanza seven introduces conflict with God and his part in all this: after all, in the following stanza it is "His frost" (the capitalization is all important) which kills the men in the night.

In terms of power the winter weather seems all powerful, but, despite the toll taken by the winter, the soldiers show a hardy resilience and Owen's very act of writing the poem shows a certain triumph of art over horrendous living conditions.

Why?

This long poem:

- gives us a vivid picture of life in the trenches in winter;

- makes clear the boredom and the lack of action that the soldiers had to endure;

- shows the horrendous, life-threatening weather conditions in the trenches;

- expresses nostalgia for their homes;

- questions both God's part in the war and the very reason the men are fighting.

'Storm on the Island' – Seamus Heaney

Context

Seamus Heaney was born on 13 April 1939 and died on 30 August 2013. Heaney was an Irish poet, widely recognized as one of the best poets writing in English in the late 20th and early 21st centuries. He was awarded the Nobel Prize for Literature in 1995. He was born and brought up in Northern Ireland, but lived in the Republic of Ireland from 1973. Heaney considers himself an Irish poet and has objected to being included in collections of 'British' poets. Northern Ireland has had a violent and troubled history, but Heaney's poems (even those which do address political concerns) are always deeply personal and rooted in everyday events and circumstances. This poem (first published in 1966 in the collection *Death of a Naturalist*) explores his relationship with nature – as do several poems in that collection.

Who? Heaney speaks as an islander awaiting a violent storm. He uses the third person plural – "we" – to suggest a community united against the threat of the storm. The poem seems addressed to a general reader.

When? In the hours before the storm hits the island. There is a strong sense of anticipation throughout the poem, as the islanders wait for the storm.

Where? On a remote island, presumably off the western coast of Ireland.

What? Heaney describes how the island is "prepared" for the storm and how its geographical features protect it from the storm's worse effects. He then discourses on the nature of the sea – and its changeability.

wizened – shrivelled-looking

stooks – a group of sheaves of grain

pummels – to strike repeatedly and heavily

strafes – bombard and harass with gunfire (usually from a plane) salvo – the simultaneous firing of artillery

Commentary

Heaney begins the poem with a confident, almost defiant, assertion; "We are prepared". The islanders' houses have been built "squat: with walls sunk into "rock" to give then added strength and resilience. The roofs are made of good slate: natural materials are used to withstand the natural phenomena of a storm. It is obvious from the rest of the poem that the island is very barren with poor soil that supports little vegetation. Heaney writes, "The wizened earth has never troubled us with hay" – which is an advantage when the storm arrives as there are no stacks or stooks of hay to be blown away by the ferocious winds of the storm. The island has no trees, so there is no danger of branches being blown off and damaging people's property. The storm and its violent noises provoke fear in the inhabitants. But there is "no natural shelter" and the islanders must sit the storm out in their houses. Because of the lack of trees the islanders cannot even distract themselves with the "leaves and branches [which] can raise a tragic chorus in a gale". The noise they can hear is the storm buffeting their own houses.

The poem is a dramatic monologue, delivered by one of the islanders. It is written in unrhymed iambic pentameters – with the exception of the opening and closing couplets which use half-rhyme – a sure sign that something is wrong. This formal structure is appropriate given the calm and organized preparedness of the opening sentence. The tone is conversational ("as you see" and "you know what I mean") and the language (until the closing few lines) is ordinary, usually monosyllabic, although Heaney conveys a sense of the power of the storm in the alliterative "blows full blast" and the onomatopoeic "pummels". Heaney makes extensive use of enjambment which also helps convey the impression of a speaking voice.

In line 12 the narrator says that "You might think the sea is company/Exploding comfortably down on the cliffs". The sea can be placid, but during the storm it "spits like a tame cat /Turned savage".

Heaney uses the onomatopoeic "exploding" in the final lines of the poem to develop an extended metaphor which compares the onslaught of the storm with a military attack on the island. The "wind <u>dives</u> and <u>strafes</u> invisibly" like fighter aircraft, space is a "<u>salvo</u>" and "We are <u>bombarded</u> with the empty air". In the midst of this attack on the island and the islanders, the speaker says "We just sit tight" – confident that their preparations will result in no lasting damage to the island. The last line of the poem does not mirror the opening sentence at all – but it does express a similar confidence and a sense of community: "Strange, it is a huge nothing that we fear", almost suggesting that what they are frightened of is nothing – given the thoroughness of their preparations.

The island itself is not a romantic idyll: it is almost completely barren and prey to extreme weather, and we might question why anybody would want to live there at all. Heaney seems to be making a point in this poem about the resilience of the human spirit and how as humans we can adapt to and survive in the most hostile environments: we are adaptable, ingenious and determined, and we are also capable of adapting ourselves to the environments that we find ourselves living in.

We can go further along this line of thinking and suggest that the poem has a symbolic quality to it. It could be argued that the storm represents all the difficulties of life – bereavement, lost love, unemployment, family discord, illness – and that such is our understanding of what might be to come – "We are prepared" – our stoicism and inner strength allow us to survive the hardships and vicissitudes of life. At the same time, the idea of a storm might refer to Great Britain's stormy relationship with Ireland over the course of centuries, and, given the date of publication, might foreshadow the Troubles to come.

Conflict and Power

Clearly in the poem the storm is a clear physical manifestation of power which will control what the islanders do while it lasts. The rain, the wind and the ferocity of the sea are all signs of the power of the storm, and Heaney emphasizes this through the extended military metaphor he uses in the final lines of the poem – as if the island were under attack from a superior military force. During its duration the storm controls the islanders – they have to "sit tight" in their homes.

However, the island and the islanders have an element of control over the storm: they have built their houses "squat" and solidly; there are no hay ricks to be blown over, no trees to be uprooted and sent crashing into houses: the islanders have adapted their lives to the island in the knowledge that it is often hit by wild and ferocious storms. They have adapted their lives and their buildings, so that, while they cannot control the storm, they can control the effects it has on the island. Through making the right preparations and by sitting tight through the storm they negate its power over them, and demonstrate their own power to survive.

This poem by Seamus Heaney about a storm:

- captures the violent essence of a storm and its effect on an isolated, barren island.

- celebrates the human ability to adapt ourselves to our environment.

- conveys the savage ferocity of the storm and the sheer power of nature.

- celebrates the human qualities of resilience, fortitude and stoicism.

- may be read in a broadly symbolic way about the individual's or the community's approach to the difficulties of life.

'Bayonet Charge' – Ted Hughes

Context

Ted Hughes was born in 1930 and died in 1998. He was one of the most famous poets of his generation and was appointed Poet Laureate in 1984 – a position he held until his death. He was born in a small village near Halifax in West Yorkshire and the landscape of his birthplace influenced him throughout his life. Hughes was a prolific poet and also wrote several books for children. His private life increased his notoriety, as his first wife (the American poet Sylvia Plath) and his next partner both committed suicide in a similar way. Much of his poetry is inspired by the power and beauty and mystery of nature. This poem, however, is perhaps influenced by the fact that Hughes's father was a First World War veteran.

Hughes' father fought in the First World War and, although the poem could be about any modern war, it is usually assumed that Hughes is writing about incidents or events that his father spoke about. The poem is written in the past tense.

Who? The poet acts as an observer and describes one unnamed man's experience of a charge towards the enemy armed with a rifle and a bayonet.

When? Unclear – it might be during the First World War. What the poem has to tell us about the experience of war is universal and applicable to all wars.

Where? A battlefield. Infantry soldiers are charging a hedge where the enemy are.

What? The poem describes the sensations of one soldier as he charges into battle.

Commentary

The poem is divided into three distinct stanzas. The first stanza describes the start of the charge towards the enemy positions. In the second the soldier seems to be frozen in time. In the final stanza the action resumes. Hughes writes in free verse and in long sentences with much use of enjambment – all this suggests the speed at which events occur in battle. There is no time to think when you are under fire and the words give us an impression of this.

With the first word - *suddenly* - we are plunged immediately into the centre of the action. As soon as the soldier awoke he was running. Hughes uses powerful harsh and vivid words to convey the experience. Everything conspires to slow him down: his sweat is heavy; he is not running but stumbling; the field is full of clods; his rifle becomes heavy

He lugged a rifle numb as a smashed arm.

The simile subtly reminding us of the dangers he faces and the assonance on *u* in *lugged/numb* gives in sound an impression of its heaviness. And all the time as he runs towards the hedge – which *dazzled with rifle fire* – around him bullets are

... smacking the belly out of the air

Smacking is onomatopoeic and we might notice that much of the imagery in this first stanza comes from the human body – *belly, arm, eye* – this soldier is being shot at and it is his body which is being attacked. In the final two lines of the stanza Hughes tells us that the patriotism which once motivated him has gone, to be replaced by *molten iron* sweating *from the centre of his chest* – another thing to slow him down.

The start of the second stanza almost comes to a stop as the soldier suffers a sense of *bewilderment*. He starts to question exactly WHY he is running towards the enemy guns:

In what cold clockwork of the stars and the nations

Was he the hand pointing that second?

The mention of the *stars* suggests that this is partly his fate to be there at that particular moment, but the *nations* reveals that this very human and individual experience is actually happening because of international politics and the habit of countries to wage war against each other. *Cold clockwork* suggests something mechanical and *cold* suggests a lack of feeling for the individual. The soldier is frozen in an appalled epiphany

... his foot hung like

Statuary in mid-stride.

The third stanza introduces a hare which appears out of the *shot-slashed furrows*: *slot-slashed* combining consonance and onomatopoeia to become very memorable. The hare is a victim of the bullets: it is clearly in agony (*rolled like a flame*) and in a state of extreme trauma and shock

... its mouth wide

Open silent, its eyes standing out.

The hare is important in the poem: on the one hand, it is symbolic of the soldier's own pain and lack of understanding; on a deeper level, Hughes uses it to suggest that was is man-made and unnatural. This is not simply to show that innocent animals can be the victims of a war; much more importantly, Hughes is suggesting that it is unnatural for human beings to take part in war too.

The soldier carries on running towards the hedge and, as he runs, he drops what Hughes calls *luxuries*

King, honour, human dignity, etcetera

He is no longer running for some of the conventional reasons that men fight. Having seen the hare and had his moment of epiphany, he is running to survive, to stay alive – no other reason. Note Hughes' dismissive use of the word *etcetera* – all the reasons given for waging war are irrelevant. Hughes ends the poem with a graphic reminder of the reality of the battlefield and the soldier's fear and his instinctive desire

To get out of that blue crackling air

His terror's touchy dynamite.

Note the onomatopoeic *crackling* and the way Hughes uses the consonance and alliteration on *t* to suggest the knife-edge of tension which the soldier feels.

This is a very powerful and physical poem dealing with the experience of the individual soldier in battle. And it IS an individual soldier – Hughes makes no mention of any other soldier being involved, so the individual's fear and isolation are given prominence.

Conflict and Power

A central conflict in this poem is all the reasons the soldier has been told or has believed he should fight – "the patriotic tear", "King, honour, human, dignity, etcetera" – and the real experience of the soldier in battle – he wants to survive! The soldier himself – through Hughes' use of verbs - possesses a certain raw human power: he "plunged past with his bayonet" and utters a "yelling alarm", but he comes into conflict with the rifle fire that "dazzled", the "Bullets smacking the belly out of the air" and the "slot-slashed furrows" caused by rifle fire – power that a lone infantryman cannot compete against. At points the soldier seems in conflict with his own equipment: he "lugged a rifle numb as a smashed arm" and his fear has a physical effect on him – he feels "molten iron" in "the centre of his chest". Ultimately the power of the enemy fire overpowers him and he simply wants to "get out of that blue crackling air". His individual power is no match for the enemy onslaught – which even comes into conflict with nature by disturbing and killing a hare. The conflict of war, despite its power, is presented by Hughes as unnatural – both for the soldier and for the hare. And the power of "King" and "honour" are presented as illusory, and certainly not worth dying for.

Why?

This interesting poem about the experience of fighting

- unusually has the moment of epiphany in the middle of the poem, not the end.

- destroys the myths about why men fight – patriotism, King and country, ecetera.

- uses harsh violent imagery to convey the soldier's fear.

- uses nature, in the form of the hare, to condemn war as unnatural.

'Remains' – Simon Armitage

Context

Simon Armitage was born in 1963 in the village of Marsden in West Yorkshire and has spent most of his life in that area. He is a very successful and highly-regarded poet, celebrated for his down-to-earth language and subject matter. His early poetry often (but not always) deals with the ordinary incidents and events of modern life and appear to be based on personal experience. However, as his career as a poet has progressed, his subject matter has widened impressively, as this poem demonstrates. 'Remains' was first published in 2008 in the collection *The Not Dead* – which was based on Armitage's interview with former British soldiers about their experiences. The poems were originally aired on a Channel 4 documentary film of the same name, shown in the summer of 2007. The poems focus on the testimonies of veterans of the Gulf, Bosnia and Malayan wars - ex-soldiers who have seldom been heard before. Armitage commented: "Never having been to the front line, turning the words, phrases and experiences of these soldiers into verse has been the closest I've ever come to writing "real" war poetry, and as close as I ever want to get."

Commentary

Who? Armitage adopts the voice of a British soldier who remembers and reflects on an incident in which he and some colleagues were sent to deal with looters raiding a bank.

When? No particular time but in the recent past.

Where? In either Iraq or Afghanistan – there is a reference to "desert sand" – but the narrator is back in the UK reflecting on his experience and the incident described in the poem.

What? Three British soldiers shoot a looter as he leaves a bank, and his dead body is removed. However, the narrator of the poem continues to be haunted by the man's bullet-ridden, bloody body.

The very opening words – *On another occasion* – suggest that we are joining an ongoing conversation and the first four stanzas tell the story of the incident in which a bank looter was killed. The soldier was acting under orders – "we got sent out/to tackle looters raiding a bank". Armitage imitates the colloquial speech of the soldier when he writes that "one of them legs it up the road" and he switches to the present tense in his telling of the anecdote about the looter. The three British soldiers open fire on the looter and the narrator vividly describes the effect of the bullets:

I see every round as it rips through his life –

I see broad daylight on the other side.

On the one hand, the way the narrator describes the dead man suggests that he is capable of empathy:

….he's there on the ground, sort of inside out,

pain itself, the image of agony.

This recognition that the looter felt "pain" and died in "agony" suggests an awareness of the looter's suffering, and such an awareness might lead to empathy or a sort of compassion. However, the casual, unfeeling treatment of the dead looter's body suggests a lack of respect for the dead: one of the narrator's mates

…tosses his guts back into his body.

Then he's carted off in the back of a lorry.

Here the verbs "tosses" and "carted off" suggest the lack of respect for the dead – he is just another dead enemy.

The first line of the next stanza marks the poem's crucial turning point. It starts with a typically brief and colloquial – *End of story* – but is followed by *except not really*: whenever the soldier goes on patrol along that street he is reminded of the man's death mainly because the road is still stained with his blood - his *blood-shadow* Armitage calls it.

Even when the soldier goes home on leave he finds the memory of the moment of the man's death comes back to haunt him: if he blinks

…he bursts again through the doors of the bank.

Sleep, and he's probably armed, and possibly not.

Dream, and he's torn apart by a dozen rounds.

The soldier tries to lose the memory through using drink and drugs to forget the murder, but they "won't flush him out"- a metaphor closely linked to military life, where to "flush out" means to force the enemy to break cover. The soldier's recourse to drink and to drugs suggests he is suffering from Post-Traumatic Stress Syndrome – or, in more prosaic terms, he cannot escape the vivid memory of the death of the looter – his body literally ripped to pieces by the rapid fire of three British soldiers.

The last seven lines of the poem build up to the climax of the last line. The soldier is haunted by the sheer vividness and stark immediacy of his memory, and his memory haunts him persistently:

he's here in my head when I close my eyes,

dug in behind enemy lines.

Armitage cleverly uses a military metaphor – *dug in* – to suggest how deep the dead man has penetrated the speaker's consciousness. The man he killed is still the enemy, but the reality of his death plagues the narrator's mind, so much so that the dead man is

not left for dead in some distant, sun-stunned, sand-smothered land

or six-feet-under in desert sand,

but near to the knuckle, here and now,

his bloody life in my bloody hands.

The climax is achieved in several ways: the last five lines are one long sentence which build to the climax of a very memorable final line; in the last four lines Armitage uses perfect rhyme at the end of three lines; one line is very long and includes the two alliterative compound adjectives – "sun-stunned, sand-smothered" – alliteration which continues in the next line with "six" and "sand". "Near to the knuckle" means close to being inappropriate – this suggests that the soldier has no control over his thoughts and memories; the line as a whole alliterates on the 'n' sound with "near", "knuckle" and "now" – which all suggest the word that is missing – "No". The last line is a perfect example of parallelism with "his bloody life" mirrored by "my bloody hands". The repetition of "bloody", along with the emphatic full rhymes, serve to stress the immediacy of the soldier's memories and the sharpness of the initial experience.

The title of the poem – "Remains" – is cleverly chosen. The poem revolves around the corpse of the dead looter – his human remains – but it also deals with what remains of the man in the soldier's life and his mind. As such his 'remains' are a constant presence which haunt the soldier, even though he is back in England.

Armitage writes in irregular stanzas of four lines with the occasional use of half-rhyme. This structure seems appropriate since military life is highly ordered and regimented, but this poem begins as a casual anecdote about the war and in the second half reveals that something is desperately wrong. That is another aspect of the poem's structure: the first four stanzas (despite their gruesome details) are light, colloquial and conversational in tone- nothing prepares us for the change that comes in the second half of the poem except perhaps the earlier use of "pain itself, the image of agony". Armitage presents the soldier's mental torment very effectively and vividly, culminating in a powerful and climactic final stanza – and he does so while retaining his use of ordinary, everyday English – there is little figurative language in this poem.

Conflict and Power

In the most obvious way the British soldiers exercise power over the looters by being able and allowed to shoot them dead on sight, but the narrator of the poem cannot control his memory or the thoughts about the dead man which plague and torment him. The gruesome physical sight of the murdered man and the memory of the incident exert power over the narrator, so that his current life is filled with traumatic memories of one man's death. His former role as a soldier is in conflict with his existence as a man.

Why?

This powerful poem written in colloquial English:

- dramatizes a violent incident from an overseas war in the words of a British soldier.

- shows strongly and vividly the long-term effects that the memory of such an incident can have on the mind of a soldier.

- clearly shows that wars can inflict mental wounds as well as physical ones.

- implies perhaps that the right and wrongs of war become irrelevant – even though he was 'right' to shoot the looter – when faced with a gruesome memory.

- presents the effects of Post-Traumatic Stress Syndrome in a personal, memorable and accessible way.

'Poppies' – Jane Weir

Context

Weir grew up on the outskirts of Manchester and works as a poet, writer and textile designer. Her poetry has been highly praised. This poem was commissioned by Carol Ann Duffy along with nine other contemporary war poems in 2009, in response to the growing violence in Afghanistan and the inquiry into the invasion of Iraq. In an interview Weir commented:

I wrote this piece from a woman's perspective, which is quite rare, as most poets who write about war have been men. As the mother of two teenage boys, I tried to put across how I might feel if they were fighting in a war zone. I was subliminally thinking of Susan Owen [mother of Wilfred Owen] *and families of soldiers killed in any war when I wrote this poem.*

Armistice Sunday – the Sunday closest to November 11th, Remembrance Day, chosen because the First World War ended on November 11th, 1918.

tucks, darts, pleats – words associated with clothes and textiles.

Who? The poet speaks directly to a son who is taking leave of his mother, the narrator.

When? We are told it is three days before Armistice Sunday, but apart from that no specific time is mentioned and no specific war is mentioned which gives the poem a universal quality. It could be any war at any time and any mother bidding farewell to her son, unsure of what will happen to him. Having said that, Armistice Sunday has only been commemorated since the First World War, and the habit of wearing poppies to remember the sacrifice of dead soldiers is also a modern phenomenon, so this is a modern poem. We know it was published in 2009.

Where? The action begins at the narrator's home and ends in the local churchyard in front of the war memorial.

What? She pins a poppy on his lapel and says goodbye at the front door. Filled with memories of his childhood, she goes to her son's bedroom and then is led to the local churchyard and the poem ends with the mother gazing at the war memorial, thinking about her son.

Commentary

The opening sentence fixes the day: it is three days before Armistice Sunday. Before her son leaves the narrator pins a poppy on the lapel of the person the poem is addressed to: it is her son, but this is only confirmed by later details. Even the gender of the speaker is not made explicit, but there are strong suggestions that it is his mother – which we will explore later. Armistice Sunday commemorates all those who have died in wars, but we might note that poppies have been placed on individual war graves to remind us that every serviceman who died was an individual. The final three lines of the first stanza use language which is rich in texture and sound qualities:

I pinned one onto your lapel, crimped petals,

spasms of paper red, disrupting a blockade

of yellow bias binding around your blazer.

Alliteration on *p* gives way to alliteration on *b*, and Weir also uses assonance to give further euphony to these lines: *pinned/crimped* and *spasms/paper/blazer* and *bias/binding*. A sense of war is introduced by the word *blockade* to describe the blazer's binding.

The second stanza gives us lots of recognizable domestic details: the mother (we assume that it is the mother because traditionally it is mothers who would fuss over a son's appearance in this way) the mother uses sellotape to remove the cat's hairs from her son's clothes and smoothes his collar down. The sellotape is *bandaged around* her hand – a hint perhaps that she is finding this leave-taking painful. The narrator says *I wanted* to rub noses with her son as they did when her son was younger, but she doesn't; she also had to resist the *impulse* to run her fingers through his hair. These details suggest that now her son is older she feels she cannot do these things that a parent might naturally do to their child when they are younger. So as our children grow up, it seems, we lose some of the intimacy we enjoyed when they were small children. Another detail which confirms that the son is older is probably the gelled blackthorns of his hair. He is old enough to make decisions about his appearance. The speaker clearly feels sad that her son is growing up: in lines 10 and 11 we are told she *steeled the softening of my face* and in line 18 she tells us *I was brave* – it is as if her face will soften with tears at her son's departure, but she manages to control her feelings in order not to embarrass her son – just as she has not rubbed noses with him or run her fingers through his hair.

The words she wants to say to him won't come; they are slowly *melting* in line 18. When she opens the front door the world is overflowing *like a treasure chest* and her son is *intoxicated*: leaving home may be sad for the parent but it can be a time of excitement and opportunity for the child as these words suggest.

As soon as he has gone she goes to his bedroom and releases a song bird from its cage; I don't think we are meant to see this as literal, but it probably symbolizes the speaker's son being released into the intoxicating, *treasure chest* world – a good thing despite his mother's obvious sadness at saying goodbye.

Weir then introduces a dove which leads the mother to the churchyard. The mother is still distracted: her stomach is busy and her nervousness about her son is conveyed to us in imagery drawn from textiles and the manufacture of clothes – *tucks, darts, pleats*; she is obviously distracted too because, although it is November, she has no coat and wears no gloves. Weir is a textile designer and often uses such vocabulary in her poems. However, the fact that she goes out improperly dressed is also a sign of her deep need to follow the dove and get to the war memorial.

Once in the churchyard the speaker traces the inscriptions on the war memorial while leaning against it *like a wishbone* – a simile that displays her fragility and which also raises the idea of wishes: presumably she would wish her son to be safe and happy. The dove flies above her and is described metaphorically as *an ornamental stitch*......... and then the poem ends

I listened, hoping to hear

Your playground voice catching on the wind.

And that phrase - *playground voice* – suggests the speaker's nostalgia for her son's childhood and her regret that he has to grow up. *Playground* is a word we associate with primary schools and it is clear from earlier details in the poem that he is older and has left childish things behind.

This is a beautiful and powerful poem. The very writing of the poem can be seen to be a political act, because Weir is writing about a topic (war) which is dominated by male poets, so to give a mother a voice is an important decision.

Some readers feel that the son is going off to war and that is why Weir is saying goodbye to him. I don't see the poem quite like that. Soldiers don't wear blazers; it is not a word used to describe what soldiers wear. I think Weir's son is going off to school – secondary school, perhaps even boarding school – and this poem is about a rite of passage for mother and for her son. A rite of passage is a ritual that marks a deep change in one's life: here it is all about sending your son off into the world, about not being able to rub noses with him because he is too old for that; it might contain the fear that later in the future he might join the army and his name might one day join the names on the war memorial.

And this fear of the future leads the mother to the war memorial, because on this day when she bids goodbye to her growing son, she feels real empathy for the mothers of the men listed on the war memorial. In their cases they said goodbye to their sons and never saw them again because they died in war. So the poppy on the lapel and the fact that this poem takes place three days before Armistice Sunday are crucial to the poem's impact. It is as if our commemoration of Armistice Sunday makes the speaker acutely aware of the much worse sacrifices that mothers make in times of war and this alerts her to what might happen in the future if her son ever becomes a soldier. Becoming a soldier (or whatever your child's first job might be) would also be a rite of passage and death is the ultimate rite of passage.

And what are we to make of the dove? It is a symbol of peace, but in the final stanza the metaphor used to describe it is an ornamental stitch, a stitch which is ornamental, not practical, not serving a purpose. Does this suggest that our hopes for peace will always be ornamental and never real, never realized, never practical? Does it suggest that war will always be with us, because the dove will remain ornamental? This may seem a little fanciful to you, but the First World War which led to so many monuments in British towns and churchyards was once thought of as the 'war to end all wars', but Weir is writing in 2009 when British soldiers were dying regularly in Afghanistan. War has continued to blight human history.

Conflict and Power

In this poem the narrator has some power over her son's appearance: she pins the poppy on his blazer, but there is a conflict between her desire to keep her son safe and his possible participation in a war in the future. However, once he has left she realizes that she has no power over war – these matters are decided by governments (although the poem does not mention this). Both the poppy and the dove are powerful symbols – one of remembrance for the dead and the other for peace - and together they draw her to the local churchyard where she traces the "inscriptions on the war memorial". She leans against the memorial "like a wishbone", showing her weakness compared with the power of the memorial and the implied power of governments in the future to send young men like her son to fight in foreign countries. There is clear conflict between her maternal instinct to keep her son safe, and the danger that in the future his name might appear on a similar war memorial. In war time, the mother would lose all control over what happens to her son – and, in fact, her position in the poem is one of powerlessness.

Why?

This interesting modern poem

- allows a woman's voice to speak on the subject of war.

- uses symbols very effectively and evocatively.

- presents an inevitable rite of passage for any mother and her child.

- links this rite of passage with the commemoration of the war dead through poppies and on Armistice Day.

- uses the language of textiles to suggest the gender of the parent.

- movingly presents the way parent/child relationships change over time.

- is more powerful because the mother in the poem represses her emotions in front of her son.

- sees the growing up of children and their loss of innocence as inevitable, but sad.

'War Photographer' – Carol Ann Duffy

Context

Carol Ann Duffy is one of the UK's most successful and best-known living poets. Her poems have a very wide appeal. On May 1st 2009 she became the nation's Poet Laureate – the first woman ever to hold the position. Her poems are often set for study by the examination boards – because they are thought of very highly and because many of them are very accessible. Her poems often use very modern and everyday language, but in fresh, funny and witty ways. She uses traditional forms like the sonnet and the dramatic monologue, but succeeds in breathing new life into these old forms by the modernity of her writing and subject matter. The accessibility of many of her poems may obscure the fact that she is highly skilled at a very intricate and ingenious manipulation of language.

Carol Ann Duffy was born in 1955 in Glasgow, but grew up in Staffordshire and studied at Liverpool University. Don McCullin was a famous photographer whose images from war-torn countries were widely published and admired. Duffy became friends with McCullin and based this poem on conversations she had with him. "War Photographer" was published in the collection *Standing Female Nude*, which appeared in 1985.

Belfast – during the period known as the Troubles, Belfast was the scene of bombings, and murders carried out by all sides in the conflict: the Provisional IRA, the Loyalist paramilitaries and the British Army.

Beirut – the capital of Lebanon and in the 70s and 80s the back-drop to a bloody civil war, sectarian violence between Christian and Islamic militias, and incursions by the Israeli Defence Force to nullify the effect of terrorist attacks on Israel. Many died.

Phnom Penh – the capital city of Cambodia. In the 1970s Cambodia was ruled by a military group known as the Khymer Rouge who massacred hundreds of thousands of their fellow citizens, an act which is now recognized as genocide.

All flesh is grass – a quotation from the Bible. Isaiah, Book 40, verse 6 reads:

All flesh is grass, and all the goodliness in us the flower of the field. The grass withereth, the flower faileth, but the word of our God shall stand forever.

The First Epistle of Peter, Book 1, verse 24 uses the same phrase. Traditionally the phrase is interpreted as showing the inevitability of death and Duffy seems to be using it ironically since in the three cities she mentions many of the violent deaths are clearly avoidable.

Who? The poem is a third person description of a war photographer (as the title makes clear), but other people are mentioned – the people he has photographed in war-torn countries, the editor of the newspaper he works for, the readers of the Sunday newspapers in which his images will appear.

When? In the late 20th century but before the use of digital cameras and the rise of social media: the photographer develops his own images in his own darkroom.

Where? The action of the poem, recounted by Duffy in the present tense, takes place in England, but the countries the photographer has visited are evoked through his memories of the suffering he has seen.

What? The photographer develops his photographs in his dark room. As the images emerge, he recalls the real life incidents that the photographs are records of. In the final stanza the photographer is flying back to some war-torn country and looks down reflectively on the United Kingdom that he is leaving behind.

In the first stanza the photographer is alone in his darkroom preparing to develop the "spools of suffering" that he has accumulated on his travels. The phrase "spools of suffering" is foregrounded by the alliteration and makes clear Duffy's sympathy for the suffering the photographer has captured in images. The photographer's role is given a quasi-sacred significance by the comparison with the priest "preparing to intone a mass" and the litany of place names of cities associated with violence. The photographer is performing a sacred task by going to dangerous places and making a photographic record, so that the rest of the world is informed about the awful suffering taking place in the world.

In the second stanza, the photographer gets to work – "He has a job to do". His hands did not tremble in the war zones, despite the danger he was in, but do so now – perhaps because of the delicacy of the task, perhaps because of the excitement of seeing the images emerge or perhaps because of the suffering that he remembers when he was taking the photographs. However, he is safe in "rural England" where he experiences only "ordinary pain" and where there are no land mines in the fields

...to explode beneath the feet

Of running children in a nightmare heat.

At the start of the third stanza – "Something is happening" – an image is emerging in the dark room. The photographer starts to see "a stranger's features" and this brings back memories of the real incident itself: "He remembers the cries/of this man's wife" and "how the blood stained into foreign dust". These memories and the way Duffy expresses them suggest a strong sense of compassion and empathy on the part of the photographer. The word "ghost" is important: it clearly suggests that the man is now dead, but it also describes the way the man slowly emerges as the photograph is developed.

In the fourth stanza we learn that he has developed "a hundred agonies in black and white" – with the word "agonies" encouraging sympathy and empathy on the part of the reader. But the reality of newspaper publishing brings us up sharply: we are told that from the "hundred agonies" he has photos of, the photographer's editor will "pick out five or six/for Sunday's supplements" – which completely ignores the majority of the "hundred agonies" and the tragic stories and suffering they bear witness to. The five or six photographs selected will "prick the tears" of the "reader's eyeballs", but will not disturb the comforting routine of the newspaper's readers – "the bath and pre-lunch beers".

The poem ends with the photographer on his way back to another war-zone:

From the aeroplane he stares impassively at where

He earns his living and they do not care.

Some readings of this poem are critical of the photographer: they stress that he regards his work as "a job" in the second stanza; his work is how he "earns his living"; and there is a sense, therefore, (it could be argued) that he makes his living from the suffering of others. However, this is to ignore the sacred religious imagery in the first stanza, the trembling of his hands in the second stanza and his vivid and clearly compassionate memories in stanza three. Besides, the photographer puts himself in positions of danger in order to tell the world what is going on in distant countries: he is performing a vital function in bringing to Western Europe's attention atrocities which may be occurring in other countries which are not often featured in the news.

If there is an object of criticism in Duffy's poem it is the British public who buy the newspapers that the photographs appear in. The British readership is safe in "Rural England", suffers "ordinary pain" which "simple weather can dispel". The readers' reaction to the photographs is "tears" – but they are not meaningful tears; they are part of a normal Sunday ritual squeezed in between a bath and "pre-lunch beers". The most searing indictment of the British public is in the last line where Duffy claims "they do not care" – they do not care about suffering in far-off foreign countries, despite the efforts of the war photographer to make them care.

Duffy chooses a very regular structure for this poem. There are four stanzas each of six lines with a final rhyming couplet and with lines two and three rhyming in each stanza. This structure seems to match the organized nature of the photographer's work – especially his meticulous work in the dark room, while the final rhyming couplet mirrors the certainty that the photographer and Duffy both feel that his work is worthwhile and fulfils an important function in society. It fills an important function in society because it brings public attention to conflicts and wars all over the world.

Conflict and Power

The photographer's job takes him to areas of conflict all over the world, but he has no power to stop the conflict – but he has the power to record it and make it known to the wider world. The poem suggests that he takes photographs of the victims of conflict – which are designed to provoke sympathy in the viewer of the photograph. However, his editor has the power to reject ninety-four of the photographs and print only six – so not every story is told, not every image is seen. He is also the recorder of the misuse of power: in Cambodia and Phnom Penh where the regime was using its power to massacre hundreds of thousands of people the world did take action, but only after the efforts of journalists had brought the regime's crimes to light. Nonetheless, the poem makes clear that there is a conflict between the whole truth (as represented by the reels of photos that the photographer takes) and the tiny number that are finally seen by the public in their newspaper. There is also a conflict between the photographer's mission to bring home the truth about overseas wars and the relative indifference of the British public.

Why?

This poem:

- encourages empathy and sympathy for all those caught up in violent conflicts all over the world.

- gives the photographer an almost sacred importance because his bravery allows images of suffering humanity to reach us.

- is an indictment of the British public for whom the photographs of suffering humanity become a part of their Sunday ritual.

- demonstrates the appalling and horrific violence of war and genocide.

- shows the relative indifference of the British public to overseas conflicts.

'Tissue' – Imtiaz Dharker

Context

Imtiaz Dharker was born in 1954 in Pakistan, but her parents emigrated to England and she grew up in Glasgow. As well as being a published poet, she is a successful film maker and book illustrator. Her work takes her between the UK and India, and she is very aware in her work of her own hybrid background, but sees it as a strength rather than a hindrance, a rich inheritance of different traditions which can coalesce rather than a source of conflict. Her poetry should be read with these contradictions in mind, as well as her desire to reconcile what she sees as trivial issues as race, background and religion.

Her collections of poems include 'Purdah' (Oxford University Press), 'Postcards from god', 'I speak for the devil' and 'The terrorist at my table (all published by Penguin India and Bloodaxe Books UK), 'Leaving Fingerprints' (Bloodaxe Books UK) and 'Over the Moon' (September 2014, Bloodaxe Books UK). Recipient of the Cholmondeley Award and a Fellow of the Royal Society of Literature, her poems are on the English GCSE and A Level English syllabus, and she reads with other poets at Poetry Live! events all over the country to more than 25,000 students a year. She has had ten solo exhibitions of drawings in India, London, New York and Hong Kong. She scripts and directs films, many of them for non-government organizations in India, working in the area of shelter, education and health for women and children.

Fine slips from grocery stops – it is not that long ago that when one paid by credit card in a shop one received a translucent slip of paper as a receipt.

Who? The poet reflects on a world made of paper which has been touched by human beings and is translucent with age. The poet appears to be speaking as herself.

When? In the present day.

Where? No precise location.

What? In a challenging poem, the poet speculates that "things" could be altered if buildings, maps and monoliths were made of tissue paper which would let the light through and which would enable us to see the truth. At the end of the poem the tissue she has been talking about is transformed into something uniquely human – human tissue – "your skin".

To make make sense of this poem it is absolutely vital to read it in the context of Dharker's other work and her other preoccupations. Coming as she does from a multi-cultural background and working as she does within two very different cultures, she is at pains in her other work to build bridges between cultures which seem – in the real world of terrorism and freedom fighters – hell bent on each other's destruction. Generalizations are sometimes loathsome, but it is no generalization to say that Dharker, in her other poems, is on the side of humanity, peace and a non-prejudiced acceptance of other people. It is with these qualities in mind that we should approach this poem.

So in a world filled with violence and hostility, with terrorism and state-sponsored terrorism, with disastrous Western military interventions in the Middle East and Afghanistan, with religious hatred and growing economic inequality, what might help? In a world of climate change and mass immigration, suicide attacks and a worldwide financial crisis, what might alter things? What might make things better? Cryptically Dharker tells us in the first stanza:

Paper that lets the light
shine through, this
is what could alter things.

It is important that the paper lets the light shine through because it is "thinned by age or touching", but the choice of paper itself is significant. The ability to produce paper – and all that follows from that: the written word, the recording of history, the writing of poetry and the transmission of knowledge – is a crucial milestone in the development of human civilization.....the very civilization that can seem threatened in these troubled times.

Dharker makes clear in the second stanza that the paper she is referring to has been used countless times by human beings – "the kind you find in well-used books" such as the family Koran

*...where a hand
has written in the name and histories,
who was born to whom,*

*the height and weight, who
died where and how, on which sepia date, pages smoothed and turned
transparent with attention.*

Not only do these lines go a long way to humanize the Muslim family who have meticulously recorded the births, the key phrase "transparent with attention" demonstrates that the paper itself has become transparent through human contact. Dharker is now going to expand on this theme of transparency and apply it to more important geo-political forces.

The next stanza speculates about buildings being made of paper – an idea the poet returns to in stanza eight. Buildings made of paper would allow the poet "to see how easily/ they fall away on a sigh". Dharker seems to be suggesting that buildings can decay and are of less ultimate importance than writing on paper.

The next stanza turns its attention to maps and significantly the "sun shines through/ their borderlines", making the borders irrelevant. Think of all the wars and conflicts in the world that are caused by disputed borders or exist between nation states (defined by their borders). Dharker seems to be appealing to our common humanity – regardless of nationality, borders, race and religion. In the next whimsical stanza Dharker imagines credit card slips flying "our lives like paper kites".

She goes on in the next stanza to claim that "Architects could use all this" translucent paper to build buildings and

...let the daylight break
through capitals and monoliths,
through the shapes that pride can make.

"Capitals and monoliths" – it is impossible not to think of all the grand government buildings and public buildings around the world – a world of borderlines which – as the poem has strongly implied – leads to conflict and war. The mention of human pride emphasises Dharker's point: pride causes wars. Instead, by using paper to make buildings architects will

find a way to trace a grand design

with living tissue

A world and a world order that is truly human and completely transparent (made of "living tissue"– where there are no secrets and where our common humanity is valued above all.

Some may argue that paper is a fragile thing – one certainly cannot make buildings from it. However, it is the way we have chosen to record our births, the shape of our world in maps, our financial transactions and the poem invests paper with more power than the "monoliths" built through pride by governments, organizations or religions. Dharker's poem is a plea for a world made human and humanized by the ordinary objects of our lives – the family Koran, the credit card slips. In a world in which even the maps become translucent and the borderlines fade, the very things which cause wars and conflict become meaningless because they can no longer be seen. The poet implies that if we were all similarly transparent about our pasts then this openness and honesty would only lead to positive results. The poem is about reclaiming power from the capitals and monoliths and relocating it in our common humanity.

Dharker imagines whole cities made of paper – more representative of humanity and human tissue than the concrete and glass monoliths built by governments or ideologies or religions. But despite the inherent fragility of paper and of human flesh, Dharker implies that together and in large quantities it is powerful – and will outlive ideologies and their monoliths. Her "message" in this poem is quite close in content to Shelley's "Ozymandias".

The form of the poem matches its content appropriately. Although arranged in four line stanzas until the final line, the poem is written in free verse – which is appropriate for the innovative ideas that Dharker is expressing. A traditional form would trap Dharker's tentative suggestions in a rigid framework; furthermore, since Dharker is arguing against the establishment view of the world, a traditional form would, in a way, be endorsing that conventional view of humanity and human power.

The end of the poem leaves us in no doubt. The final line is foregrounded by being isolated at the end of the poem and Dharker imagines that the "paper smoothed and stroked/ and thinned to be transparent" has "turned into your skin" (playing on the other meaning of "tissue" as human flesh). This ending, together with the poem's frequent use of the images of light and transparency, is of a world made better by being both transparency and a humanized way of ordering our affairs.. A recognition of our common humanity and a rejection of "capitals and monoliths" might be "what could alter things" and make the world a better place.

Conflict and Power

The issues of conflict and power may seem less clear cut in this poem. However, if we see power residing in the "capitals" and "monoliths" – the grand buildings which are built by human pride in the service of state power or some ideology or religion, then (within the world of the poem) these structures (and the unbending and intransigent ideas they promote) are in clear conflict with buildings made of translucent paper. Dharker's idea may be far-fetched and slightly whimsical but it is on the side of the human, the personal, the paper made translucent by repeated human use over many generations and against the "monoliths" that would seek to control us and use us. Dharker seems to be suggesting that human beings and the paper touched by human beings has the power to take on and defeat – through transparency and light, the monoliths built by human pride.

Why?

This whimsical, but deeply serious poem:

- imagines a world made of paper touched and worn thin by contact with human hands.

- imagines that in such a world the capitals and monoliths of organized government and religion would be replaced by lightness and transparency.

- strongly implies that the lightness and transparency would start to "alter things" and begin to lead to a world without conflict or hatred or dogmatism.

- locates real power in the humanity of used paper rather than the monoliths that really control us.

'The Emigrée' – Carol Rumens

Context

Carol Rumens was born in South London. She won a scholarship to grammar school and later studied Philosophy at London University, but left before completing her degree. She gained a Postgraduate Diploma in Writing for the Stage (with Distinction) from City College Manchester in 2001. She taught at University of Kent at Canterbury (1983-5), Queen's University Belfast (1991-3 and 1995-8)), University College Cork (1994), University of Stockholm (1999), and University of Hull. As visiting Professor of Creative Writing, she now teaches at the University of Wales, Bangor, and the University of Hull. Rumens' long-time partner is a Russian who defected from the USSR and she has shown great interest in Russia and Eastern Europe, visiting several time – both before and after the fall of Communism – and editing and translating the work of Russian poets.

Given Ruben's interest in Eastern Europe and the defection of her Russian partner to the West, it is tempting to read this poem as being about an emigrée from the Soviet Union. However, one of the strengths of the poem is that it does not deal in such details and, therefore, stands as a statement – a very positive statement in the end – of the plight of any political refugee from any repressive political system. The emigrée can be seen as being from any eastern European state – after all, Berlin (now the capital of Germany) had a physical wall which separated the Communist East from the Capitalist West. Interestingly, the poem and its childlike voice pay little attention to political repression (although it is mentioned) and prefers to develop the speaker's relationship with the city she has had to leave and which is associated throughout the poem with sunlight – a hopeful and optimistic view of the future. The tone of the speaker remains naïve and child-like throughout the poem, and this tone may be to suggest the speaker's difficulty in speaking English, but is more likely be a way of conveying an essential optimism about the future of her city.

At the end of the Second World War the USSR ensured that there were Communist governments in the eastern European countries that they had liberated. The Soviet Union clearly wanted a buffer zone: the German invasion of the USSR during the Second World War has caused 27 million Russian deaths and many towns and villages in Russia had been destroyed. However, life for ordinary people in Eastern Europe was bleak: they had no democracy and critics of the Communist system were persecuted and treated harshly by the authorities. In addition, because the USSR spent so much money on its military, ordinary citizens in Eastern Europe had a standard of living that was much lower than in Western Europe: Eastern Europeans had no freedom of speech and no cars and no fridges. They were not allowed to travel freely to foreign countries. Many chose to defect to the West to enjoy a better standard of living and to enjoy freedom of speech and expression. Poets, writers and dissidents who criticized the regime were often send to the Soviet labour camp system or had their writings banned. It was a repressive political system.

The fall of the Berlin Wall in the autumn of 1989 signalled the break-up of the Communist system, and now democracy and free speech have returned to Eastern Europe. The former Soviet Union was formally dissolved in 1991.

The Emigrée – the French-derived word with an extra 'e' on the end tells us that this poem is about a woman who has left her native country. The woman is the speaker in the poem.

a hollow doll – perhaps a reference to the famous Matroyushka dolls so popular in Russia.

Who? Rumens adopts the persona of a women who is in exile from her home city, apparently in Eastern Europe.

When? This poem was published in 1993 shortly after the fall of Communism and the liberation of Eastern Europe from Soviet tyranny.

Where? Although the woman is in exile, so much of the poem is about the city she left behind and it is evoked so vividly that her home city could be said to be the location of the poem.

What? The speaker of the poem reflects with joy and nostalgia about her home city from which is in exile, but also introduces negative imagery which suggests that life in her home city is oppressive and not free.

Commentary

The poem begins almost like a fairy story – "There once as a country" – but the speaker tells us "I left it as a child" – and the poem has a slightly child-like tone to it, even when it is discussing very serious matters. Her memories of the city are positive and associated with its being "sunlight clear" – the motif of sunlight runs all the way through the poem. Even the "worst news" that she sometimes hears from the city cannot break her original view of the city as a "bright, filled paperweight".

It may be at war, it may be sick with tyrants,
but I am branded by an impression of sunlight.

"Branded" is an interesting choice of word: we brand livestock – cattle and sheep – to show who they belong to, so it is as if the speaker still belongs to her native city despite her long exile. The last word of each stanza is "sunlight" which not only reflects her strongly positive feelings towards her native city, but also suggests that change is on the way and she may be able to return despite the "city of walls" in the final stanza which mutters death.

Rumens presents the city as attractive: in the second stanza it is described as having "white streets" and "graceful slopes" which "glow". She then employs a very interesting metaphor – she writes that time "rolls its tanks". This would appear to mean that time is increasing the barriers between her and her home city, but the simile of rolling tanks is full of resonance for anyone who lived through the Cold War. Hungary in 1956 and Czechoslovakia in 1968 both rebelled against Soviet Communist rule and the Russians responded by sending in tanks and troops – with a particular focus being the capital cities of Budapest and Prague. This was the usual Russian response to political protest in Eastern Europe. Rumens continues the simile by writing "the frontiers rise between us, close like waves" suggesting still further her isolation and exclusion from her home city – because of the physical difficulty of visiting it. The implication is clear – "frontiers" which divide and separate human beings are potentially evil constructs.

One thing she did manage to bring with her from her city is her language the "child's vocabulary" that I "carried here/like a hollow doll" – a simile which reinforces the connection with Russia, famous for its matroyushka, the hollow dolls which contain smaller and smaller dolls. Her memory of her native language seems to possess a power of its own – it "spills a grammar" – and the speaker is determined and defiant to retain her language despite the restrictions of the state:

It may by now be a lie, banned by the state,
but I can't get it off my tongue.

And besides her vocabulary "tastes of sunlight", thus continuing the generally positive and optimistic tone of the poem. The Russian authorities regularly banned books and even words during the Cold War, and it was possible for writers and poets to be imprisoned for what they had written if it offended the totalitarian governments of eastern Europe.

The third stanza opens with a plaintive admission:

I have no passport, there's no way back at all
But in a fantasy sequence the speaker's comes to me in "its own white plane". The speaker cossets it and fusses over it as if it were a long-lost child:

It lies down in front of me, docile as paper;
I comb its hair and love its shining eyes.

Then, in what should be a life-enhancing moment, "my city takes me dancing" – however, she takes the speaker dancing through the ominously-sounding "city of walls". Walls are built to keep people out or to keep things hidden and secret. The "city of walls" seems to represent all the dark forces of repression and oppression that we associate with the former Soviet Union and its eastern European allies.. In the poem the walls accuse the speaker of absence and they circle her in a threatening manner. Her own city is intimidated and "hides behind me", while the city of walls "mutters death" and in the final line "my shadow falls as evidence of sunlight". The word "shadow" introduces a note of darkness into the poem but, overall, the shadow exists "as evidence of sunlight", so the final stanza, like the first two, ends with the word "sunlight" and a sense of optimism for the future.

The form of the poem is measured and controlled: two eight line stanza, followed by a final nine line stanza – the extra line perhaps representing some hope for change. Each line is roughly the same length and the measured tome reflects the calmness of the narrator who recounts very traumatic events and feelings in a measured and stoical way. Perhaps this is a deliberate ploy on Ruben's part to suggest either the quiet determination of the speaker or her unfamiliarity with English - we have commented already on the almost child-like voice of the poem's speaker – or perhaps both.

Conflict and Power

The central conflict of the poem is that between the emigrée and the country she has been forced to flee, made all the more moving because she cannot return to her home city and feels intense nostalgia for it. The government of the speaker's native country has the power to force her to emigrate in search of freedom. It can also ban words and allow the tanks to roll across national frontiers when it does not get its own way or when it feels threatened. The "city of walls" that mutters death in the final stanza seems to be the continuing threat of repression which engenders fear.

However, that is only one part of the poem. Despite being exiled from her city, the speaker speaks of it with enormous affection and pays it loving attention when reunited with it. The final stanza may include the sinister "city of walls", but the poem ends on the word "sunlight". This expresses hope that repression and oppression will eventually be gone as the authoritarian Communist state is dismantled.

Why?

This poem:

- highlights the plight of the emigrée in exile from her native city.

- makes it clear from the tanks and the banning of language that the city is in an authoritarian country that does not allow freedom of expression or dissent.

- emphasizes the deracination that the speaker feels away from her native city.

- expresses the speaker's joy at being reunited with her city.

- ends on a note of optimism – the city of walls may mutter death but the final word of the poem (and of every stanza) is "sunlight". Perhaps sunlight represents the irresistible human urge for freedom and free expression.

'Kamikaze' – Beatrice Garland

Context

Beatrice Garland was born in Oxford in 1938 and works as an NHS clinician and researcher. In 2001 she won the National Poetry Prize. She also won the Strokesdown International Poetry Competition in 2002 and was short-listed for the first Picador Poetry Prize.

Towards the end of the Second World War, Japan was losing the war against American forces who were steadily advancing towards the Japanese home islands. To defend Japan special units of the Japanese air force were formed, known as kamikaze pilots (the name literally means "Divine Wind"); their official name was Special Attack Unit. Japan had lost its naval superiority by late 1944 and the kamikaze pilot's job was to destroy American ships by deliberately crashing their planes into American warships and in doing so, losing their own lives. Kamikaze pilots were on suicide missions, prepared to sacrifice their lives for the defence of Japan. Their sacrifice was seen both as a religious and a patriotic obligation. The planes the kamikaze pilots flew were specially adapted and packed with explosive materials in order to maximize damage to the American ships. Kamikaze pilots who failed to complete their mission – for whatever reason – were ostracized after the war and held in contempt for their failure to kill themselves for the sake of Japan.

To understand why the failed pilots were ostracized it is important to understand the Japanese attitudes to suicide. In Europe suicide has, for centuries, been condemned by the church as a sinful and selfish act. By contrast, suicide in Japan has a long and honourable tradition dating back many centuries. In Japan suicide has been seen as an acceptable response to failure or defeat in battle. In Japanese society an individual's identity is not valued as much as acceptance by society and conformity to society's mores. Therefore, how you are perceived by others is very important. If one feels ostracized or alienated from one's society, then suicide is still seen in Japanese culture as an acceptable response.

Who? Beatrice Garland writes in the third person about a failed Kamikaze pilot and his family's reaction to him. However, she writes from the perspectives of both the wife and the daughter of the Kamikaze pilot and at points in the poem she slips once into the direct voice of the man's daughter who tells his story to her own children.

When? At an indeterminate point after the Second World War, although much of the poem's description is of things the man saw on the day he flew his Kamikaze mission in 1944 or 1945.

Where? In Japan.

What? The Kamikaze pilot sets off for his mission, but half-way there he changes his mind and returns home, having failed to carry out his suicide mission. On his return his daughter never speaks to him again and his neighbours "treated him/as though he no longer he existed".

Commentary

In the first stanza Garland describes how the girl's grandfather "embarked at sunrise"

With a flask of water, a samurai sword

In the cockpit, a shaven head

Full of powerful incantations

And enough fuel for a one-way

Journey into history.

The voice of the second stanza shifts to the daughter of the pilot who is "recounting it later to her children", and the next four stanzas explore (through the daughter's speculation) what made him fail to complete his mission. As he flew over the sea, she imagines, he must have looked down at the sea and seen the

...little fishing boats

strung out like bunting

on a green-blue translucent sea

and under the water he might have seen

the dark shoals of fishes

flashing silver as their bellies

swivelled towards the sun

The importance of the descriptions of the sea and the fish in stanzas two and three is that they make the natural world seem so attractive and wonderful – it makes the pilot's decision not to commit suicide more understandable. Life is precious and the teeming and beautiful life of the sea underlines this fact.

The fourth stanza speculates about whether he remembered waiting with his brothers on the beach for his father's boat to return: this detail gives more significance to stanzas two and three: the pilot comes from a fishing family so he will be naturally drawn to the sea and the sight of fish. His father would return safe to the shore, and there is a vivid and memorable description of his catch:

...cloud-marked mackerel,

black crabs, feathery prawns,

the loose silver of whitebait and once

a tuna, the dark prince, muscular, dangerous.

The associations of words like "silver" and "prince" suggest that the life of a simple fisherman has unexpected blessings, and the whole stanza exudes a sense of the rich harvest of the sea. Like the descriptions of the sea in the second and third stanzas, the evocative descriptions of the catch make it clear that the pilot simply wanted to be a fisherman like his father and to enjoy the pleasures and plenitude of life.

Garland switches narrator in stanza six to one of the man's children. She tells us that "mother never spoke again in his presence" and that the neighbours "treated him/as though he no longer existed". However, the man's children do not understand the mores of their culture and "we children still chattered and laughed". However, in time even the children became aware of their father's 'crime'

....we too learned

to be silent, to live as though

he had never returned, that this

was no longer the father we loved.

As the children grow more aware of Japanese traditions, they copy the adults around him and do not communicate with him at all.

Garland gives the closing words of the poem to the man's wife:

And sometimes, she said, he must have wondered

which had been the better way to die.

Whether the man would have been happier if he had died in the war on his suicide mission than living but living in a society where no one speaks to him, not even his own family. But this is speculation – in the poem we do not hear from the man himself – only from his wife and daughter. It is as though the poem itself mimics Japanese society by denying the man any communication. The poem ends on a note of sadness by comparing the man's life to a living death, but at the centre of the poem is the vivid description of his father's fishing haul – perhaps suggesting the centrality and importance of all that teeming marine life to the man.

The form of the poem is very regular: it is set out in seven unrhymed stanzas of roughly equal lines. This seems to be appropriate to mirror the formal nature of Japanese society in which the husband is ostracized by **his own children** for not committing suicide in the war and in which what he did in the war is simply not referred to by anyone.. However, despite the final words of the wife – which suggest the man is living a life which is like a death – the overall tone of the poem is elegant and graceful which strongly suggest that the man – in choosing life, has chosen correctly, despite the condemnation of his family and his society.

Conflict and Power

It cannot be disputed that Japanese social attitudes are presented by Garland as very powerful in this poem: as the man's children grow up they adopt the traditional attitudes of their society and ignore their own father. We might say that the man's desire to live puts him in conflict with the accepted traditions of his society. However true that is – and Garland presents the man's experience as the central narrative of the poem – there are other forces at work in the poem. As the man looks down at the sea as he begins his mission, he is reminded of his childhood and the excitement he felt at his father's fishing haul: the failed kamikaze pilot's memory is strong and is in conflict with his patriotic duty. Equally powerful is Garland's presentation of his children's innocence: they treat their father normally until they learn they are not supposed to. It is not hard for the sensitive reader to question the power of Japanese social conventions – especially as it ruins the children's relationship with their father. In the third stanza Garland uses an interesting and evocative simile: she describes the would-be kamikaze pilot looking down at the sea and seeing "the dark shoals of fishes"

like a huge flag waved first one way

then the other in a figure of eight

It is as if the man has rejected his national flag – flags represent countries and men die for their countries in war – for this figurative flag of fishes and the sheer beauty of the sea. Since the man in the poem is never given a voice (much as he is ignored by his society), we can only assume that – despite his ostracism – he is happy with his choice. Garland's language when she describes the natural world suggest that this may be so.

Why?

This beautifully expressed poem vividly presents:

- a society with rigid traditions which lead to one man's complete ostracism from his family and his neighbours.

- the beauty and plenitude of the natural world.

- the power of human memory.

- the power of life and a love of life when faced with death.

- the determination of one man to live, despite the disapproval of his society.

'Checking Out Me History' – John Agard

Context

John Agard was born in the former British colony of Guyana in 1949 and he has written many books for children and adults. He moved to Britain in 1977 and lives in Sussex with his partner Grace Nichols – who is also a poet. Agard is well-known as a skilled and adept performer of his own poems and you may get the chance to see him perform his poems during your course. You should check out his performance of the poem 'Half-Caste' on YouTube, because his performance helps to bring the poem alive. In many of his poems he uses Caribbean accent and dialect to bring a Guyanese identity to his work, but he also uses Standard English in some poems.

This poem mentions certain historical figures and it is important to know who they are.

1066 is a crucial date in English history because it marked the start of the Norman/French takeover of British society, the destruction of Anglo-Saxon society and the introduction of the feudal system.

Dick Whittington is a figure from English legend – a poor boy (with nothing apart from a cat) who became Mayor of London and is the subject of fairy tales and pantomimes.

Toussaint L'Ouverture (1743 – 1803) was the black leader of the Haitian revolution against French colonial rule. He abolished slavery in Haiti and turned it into an independent republic.

Nanny de Maroon – Maroons is a general term used to describe black slaves brought to European colonies in the West Indies and South America who escaped from slavery and then lived in remote areas of the jungle in the colonies to which they had been transported. Nanny de Maroon (1700 – 1740) is the only woman who has been proclaimed a hero of Jamaican history. She was a real historical figure who led the

Maroons on Jamaica in a rebellion against British rule. She organized many slave escapes, led the maroons to victory in various battles against British troops and finally won improvements in the way slaves were treated in the plantations on the island.

Lord Horatio Nelson was a famous English admiral who inflicted a massive defeat on the French navy at the sea battle of Trafalgar in 1805. Although Nelson was killed in the course of the battle, he became a national hero and his destruction of the French navy resulted in the strengthening and extension of the British Empire.

The Battle of Waterloo in 1815 was the final defeat of the French army led by Napoleon. It confirmed Britain's status as the world's first super-power.

Shaka (1787 – 1828) was an influential leader of the Zulu nation. He united the Zulu people against other tribes and the increasing presence of white settlers, and made important innovations in battle tactics and new weaponry.

Caribs and Arawaks were the original inhabitants of the West Indies at the time that Columbus 'discovered' the islands. They were killed off either by war or through exposure to European diseases to which they had no immunity. 'Discovered' is in inverted commas there, because he only discovered it for Europeans; the islands and their inhabitants were already there!

Florence Nightingale (1820 – 1910) was a famous British nurse. She became legendary for her work in the Crimean War and for her innovations in hygiene and in post-operative care of patients.

Robin Hood was a legendary English hero, famed for fighting unjust authority (represented by the Sheriff of Nottingham) and for stealing money from the rich and giving it to the poor.

Mary Seacole (1805 – 1881) was a Jamaican woman who travelled to the Crimea to tend to wounded British soldiers in the same way as Florence

Nightingale did. In her lifetime Seacole was as well-known as Nightingale, but she gradually faded from public memory. More recently, however, through writers such as Agard, she has been remembered again as an example of a heroic black woman who made a unique contribution to our history.

The Crimean War (1854 – 56) was fought between the Russian Empire on one side and Britain, France and the Ottoman Empire on the other. Most of the fighting took place on the Crimean Peninsula (which is part of Russia). The concentration of large numbers of troops in a relatively small area led to outbreaks of diseases such as cholera and, combined with poor supplies of food, resulted in many unnecessary deaths. At the start of the war the hospital facilities were inadequate and very unclean – a situation which Florence Nightingale did much to improve.

Agard also makes allusions to various well-known English nursery rhymes: 'The Cow Jumped Over the Moon' and 'Old King Cole'.

Dem – they

me – my

bout – about

dat – that

lick back – defeated

de – of

see-far woman – a woman who had a vision of how escaped slaves might live more freely

Who? Agard speaks as himself protesting about the way black culture and history have been ignored or marginalized.

When? The poem is set in the present day, but looks back at the education system in Guyana and in the UK.

Where? There is no specific location.

What? Throughout the poem we alternate between lines full of references to white Europeans and their culture with different stanzas celebrating the achievements of black men and women.

Commentary

Agard was born in Guyana and this poem explores the contrast between the history that everyone is taught in schools and is common or general knowledge, and the history that is not widely taught or known about. The 'official' versions if history are filled with white people because, Agard and many others would say, history has been written by white people and it deliberately excludes famous black men and women who have had a remarkable effect on history or who deserve to be more widely recognized.

In the first stanza Agard begins with simple repetition. The tone is accusatory and angry:

Dem tell me

Dem tell me

What dem want to tell me

Those three words – *Dem tell me* – are going to be used at the start of all the four line stanzas that rhyme. The repetition serves to emphasize the control that white society has over history. If you control the knowledge of the past, then you can control how people think and, more importantly, how they think about themselves, their sense of self-esteem and pride. Agard presents this distortion of history as a deliberate act in lines 4 and 5

Bandage up me eye with me own history

Blind me to me own identity

The alliteration on *b* at the start of each line suggests that this distortion of history is destructive and deliberate. Agard's choice of language in this poem is significant. In other poems he uses standard English, but it is appropriate that he should use spelling which imitates the way he speaks in this poem. The poem is all about his true identity – as revealed in the forgotten but heroes black figures of history; his voice is also part of his identity, reflecting his culture and background.

Line 6 begins a quatrain which is repeated in different words throughout the poem. In each quatrain Agard begins by mentioning famous white figures from British history and usually ends the quatrain with some mention of a black historical figure who is left out of the historical accounts. But there is more going on than that. The style of the quatrains with their predictable rhymes emphasize the childishness of what he has been told about the past and, as well as mentioning white heroes from British history, he also mentions characters from nursery rhymes and myth. The effect of all this is to mock what he has been told about the past and the attitudes of those who seek to ignore or marginalize black achievements.

Interspersed with these quatrains are longer verses which concentrate, in turn, on someone famous and remarkable from black history: Toussaint L'Ouverture, Nanny de Maroon and Mary Seacole. What is really important though is the way these verses are written: they lack the tone of mockery of the quatrains, partly because they do not rhyme; they are italicized so that they stand out visually; the lines are shorter; they are written in free verse which is appropriate because Agard is using an unconventional form to introduce unconventional ideas. Agard does use some rhyme but not in the highly regular way he does in the quatrains, so the language does not feel predictable. Also they are filled with metaphor and positive imagery to convince us of the extraordinary nature of the figures that Agard chooses to write about. Here is the verse about Nanny de Maroon

Nanny

see-far woman

of mountain dream

fire-woman struggle

hopeful stream

to freedom river

This uses language in unusual and original ways and original compound adjectives – *see-far, fire-woman* – because Agard is introducing unusual people whom we may not have heard of and his use of ellipsis makes her achievements sound extraordinary. In a similar way the metaphor used to describe Mary Seacole is full of hope and promise:

a yellow sunrise

to the dying.

You might note too that nowhere in the poem does Agard use any punctuation – it is as if the rules of punctuation – like the white version of history - is something he chooses to reject, because it threatens his identity and imposes someone else's rules on him.

In the final stanza he angrily points out again that

Dem tell me wha dem want to tell me

but now he knows about Toussaint, Nanny and Mary Seacole he is able to carve out his own identity and reclaim his pride.

Conflict and Power

This poem protests against the power of the white establishment which excludes black heroes from history lessons. Agard's poem is both a protest against this exclusion, but also an attempt to make his readers aware of important figures from black history who are admirable or outstanding in some way. The poem makes clear that the exclusion of important black figures from our history is a source of conflict because it deliberately excludes important or significant black historical figures. This exclusion is presented by Agard as wrong.

Why?

This cleverly constructed poem

- uses a distinctive voice to reclaim black identity from the official white versions of history.

- makes the reader aware of our own assumptions about British history.

- introduces us to famous black men and women who achieved extraordinary things and acts as a memorial to them.

- rehabilitates the memory of black men and women who made extraordinary contributions to human history.

- reminds us that who controls the past controls the present.

- cleverly uses two types of stanza in order to underline the differences between the official version of history and the alternative view of the past.

- demonstrates that without a history and without a distinctive voice we may have no identity.

LOVE & RELATIONSHIPS

'When We Two Parted' – George Gordon, Lord Byron

Context

Byron was the ideal of the Romantic poet, gaining notoriety for his scandalous private life and being described by one contemporary as 'mad, bad and dangerous to know'. George Gordon Noel, sixth Baron Byron, was born on 22 January 1788 in London. His father died when he was three, with the result that he inherited his title from his great uncle in 1798.

Byron spent his early years in Aberdeen, and was educated at Harrow School and Cambridge University. In 1809, he left for a two-year tour of a number of Mediterranean countries. He returned to England in 1811, and in 1812 the first two cantos of 'Childe Harold's Pilgrimage' were published. Byron became famous overnight. His other works of this period 'The Corsair' and 'Hebrew Melodies' sold very well and Byron became a celebrity in fashionable society and the toast of London society. There is a case for thinking of him as the first celebrity poet.

In 1814, Byron's half-sister Augusta gave birth to a daughter, almost certainly Byron's. The following year Byron married Annabella Milbanke, with whom he had a daughter, his only legitimate child. The couple separated in 1816, in controversial circumstances – Byron being accused by his wife of 'unnatural practices'.

The furore over his marriage and his tangled love life led London society to shun him. Facing mounting pressure as a result of his failed marriage, scandalous affairs and huge debts, Byron left England in April 1816 and never returned. He spent the summer of 1816 at Lake Geneva with Percy Bysshe Shelley, his wife Mary and Mary's half-sister Claire Clairmont, with whom Byron had a daughter.

Byron travelled on to Italy, where he was to live for more than six years. In 1819, while staying in Venice, he began an affair with Teresa Guiccioli, the wife of an Italian nobleman. It was in this period that Byron wrote some of his most famous works, including 'Don Juan' (1819-1824).

In July 1823, Byron left Italy to join the Greek insurgents who were fighting a war of independence against the Ottoman Empire. On 19 April 1824 he died from fever at Missolonghi, in modern day Greece. His death was mourned throughout Britain. His body was brought back to England and buried at his ancestral home in Nottinghamshire.

sever – to cut through

knell – the bell that is sounded when someone has died.

rue - regret

Who? Byron (whom we assume to be the speaker in the poem) and an unnamed lady with whom he had an affair – often thought to be Lady Frances Wedderburn Webster. The poem is addressed to his former lover.

When? The poem was first published in 1816. Byron uses the present tense, but also shifts to the past tense in writing about their relationship and the way it ended.

Where? No specific location.

What? Byron laments the ending of the relationship and claims it still has the power to affect him on a deep emotional level.

Commentary

Byron is reflecting in poetry on a relationship that failed. The lovers have parted in 'silence and tears' and their separation has lasted for years: they have been severed 'for years'. At the time of their parting his lover's cheek grew cold and her kiss even colder; the last two lines of the first stanza show that the speaker still feels sorrow and anguish over their parting, feelings that still consume him in the present:

Truly that hour foretold

Sorrow to this.

When they parted the speaker felt the morning dew 'chill on my brow' and the pain of parting is something he feels even now:

It felt like a warning

Of what I feel now.

The third stanza introduces a mystery. He accuses his former lover of having broken all her vows and states that her fame is 'light' – not good: it implies that breaking her vows has led to a loss of reputation and social scandal. The speaker hears his lover's name spoken and he shares 'in its shame'. However, it is not made completely clear what that shame is nor why the speaker should share in it.

When his lover's name is mentioned in his hearing it is like a 'knell in mine ear'. However, no one knew of their relationship:

They know not that I knew thee,

Who knew thee too well.

How can you know someone too well? Perhaps their intimacy has been so intense that it pains him to think of what he has lost; alternatively, perhaps the poet knew she would break her vows. Byron ends the verse asserting through repetition how deeply he regrets the end of their relationship, so much so that he cannot describe his feelings in words:

Long, long shall I rue thee,

Too deeply to tell.

The final stanza's first two lines are bound together by alliteration on the second word of each line:

In secret we met,

In silence I grieve –

And the 'we' of the first line balances the 'I' of the second; the first line is in the past tense – the second line in the present. Byron's feelings of sadness are that his former lover could forget him ('thy heart could forget') and that she has in some way deceived him ('Thy spirit deceive'). In the final four lines Byron states that if they should meet now after so many years apart he would greet her 'With silence and tears', showing that the pain of the ending of the relationship continues and verbally reminding us of the second line of the poem – nothing has changed since the day they parted. Byron still feels intense sorrow at their parting.

Byron uses a strict rhyme scheme and generally each line has two stressed syllables. He chooses words that are mainly monosyllabic. The short words, the short lines and the regular rhyme scheme (ABABCDCD) give Byron a formal control over the poem, but paradoxically hint at turbulent emotions below the surface which are controlled and held back by the formal aspects of the construction of the poem. This paradox, in its turn, means that the poem we are left with is deeply felt and moving – because the words, lines and rhyme scheme are so tightly controlled. It's almost as if Byron cannot trust himself to be more expansive or his emotions would burst forth in an unrestrained muddle… so the control he exercises in the poem is a deliberate ploy to help restrain and control intense emotions.

Overall this is a sad and bitter poem, and one that is not really concerned with Byron's lover at all: it is more concerned with her effect on him and the enduring sense of loss he feels at their separation.

Although first published in 1816, Byron said that he wrote the poem in 1808 in order to protect the identity of the woman he was writing about. Lady Francis Wedderburn Webster was linked romantically to the Duke of Wellington, and poem describes Byron's emotional state at the end of his secret relationship with Lady Frances and her rejection of him for the Duke of Wellington. Her affair with the Duke scandalized society, but Byron in the poem is scrupulous in keeping her identity a secret.

A Romantic Poem?

The relatively simple diction and the very simple form – only two stressed syllables per line make this a typically Romantic poem. It is also Romantic because it deals with intimate, intense personal feelings. These characteristics mark it out as different from the poetry that immediately preceded it.

Byron's 'When We Two Parted':

- is a poem of intense emotion and heart-break;

- uses a short metre and relatively simple vocabulary to express his feelings – even claiming at one point that he cannot find the words he needs;

- the rigid control of the rhyme scheme and metre suggest passionate feelings which are being kept under control;

- uses the past and present tenses in a masterful way – to suggest the effect of their initial break up and its continuing source of pain to Byron.

'Love's Philosophy' – Percy Shelley

Context

Percy Bysshe Shelley was born in 1792 and drowned in a boating accident just before his 30th birthday in 1822. He lived in turbulent times: the French Revolution had begun in 1789 and in Britain the Industrial Revolution was changing the country in deep and lasting ways. Shelley was quite a rebel – and was a political radical. He sympathized with the ideas behind the French Revolution and wanted to see greater change in Britain – more democracy, more freedom, less oppression. You should remember that although Britain was an enormously wealthy nation (because of the Industrial Revolution and the huge expanse of the British Empire), the majority of the population lived in appalling poverty and most adults did not have the vote – the right to vote was limited to those who owned a certain amount of property and was, therefore, limited to a tiny minority of adult males. It was not until 1928 that all men (regardless of what they owned) were able to vote. This poem, however, has no political resonances.

fountains – natural springs of water, not man-made fountains.

mingle – mix together.

clasp – embrace

disdained – scorned, rejected, looked down upon.

Who? The speaker (whom we may assume is Shelley) attempts to persuade a woman to love him and to kiss him.

When? The poem was published in 1820.

Where? There is no specific location.

What? The poet uses a series of examples from nature of things which mix, mingle or join together in order to persuade the woman to love him.

Commentary

This short and simple poem has a rather grand title – 'Love's Philosophy' – and we will see by the end of this commentary that Shelley's ideas do have a basis in a very serious view of humanity's relationship with nature and the Romantic view of nature.

The first stanza begins by listing things in nature that are intimately connected:

The fountains mingle with the river

And the rivers with the ocean.

The winds of heaven mix for ever

With a sweet emotion.

The opening stanza avoids using any plosive consonants – there is a preponderance of 'm's and 'w's and the gentle tone is enhanced by the feminine rhyme which Shelley uses in the first seven lines of the first stanza. The effect is also enhanced by Shelley's use of personification which leads naturally to his conclusion (he is, after all writing a poem to persuade a woman to love him):

Nothing in the world is single,

All things by a law divine

In another's being mingle –

So why not I with thine?

The feminine line endings continue until the final line of the stanza which ends on a clear masculine ending – 'thine'. Shelley is arguing that there is a universal law that everything in nature is connected and the personification in the first verse is carried by the verbs 'mix' and 'mingle' and 'mingle' is repeated in line 1 and line 7.

The second stanza continues with more examples from nature, but Shelley's vocabulary is more loving and romantic. Personification is used throughout as it is in the first stanza, but the verbs are more passionate and more obviously connected to romantic love:

See the mountains <u>kiss</u> high heaven.

And the waves <u>clasp</u> one another.

'Kiss and 'clasp' will be repeated at the end of the stanza and in the first half of the second stanza Shelley continues to use feminine rhyme, which makes the poem more tentative and less forceful as befits a persuasive poem. However, line 13 marks a change to masculine rhymes and the tone of the poem becomes more confident as a result:

And the sunlight clasps the earth,

And the moonbeams kiss the sea –

What is all this sweet work worth,

If thou kiss not me?

Interestingly, both stanzas end with a rhetorical question and the final line of each stanza is made up of monosyllabic words – as if implying that the answer to the question is simple – the lovers should follow all the examples that Shelley gives from nature and kiss and clasp one another. This is Shelley's argument: we are surrounded by pairs of things which mingle and kiss and we should follow their example. His use of a regular stanza enhances the notion that this is a logical argument: two stanzas of eight lines each with a matching rhyme scheme – ABABCDCD.

All the examples Shelley uses from nature are personified and in all of the examples he sees examples of love, harmony and intimacy. This could be seen as a sort of extended example of pathetic fallacy where one's natural surroundings reflect one's feelings and emotions.

Some readers are critical of Shelley's title, arguing that the poem does not set out a philosophy at all. However, if we look at Romantic ideas about the world and science, we will find a close correlation between the poem's presentation of the natural world and the principles of Romantic science.

Romanticism had four basic principles: the original unity of man and nature in a Golden Age; the subsequent separation of man from nature and the fragmentation of human faculties; the interpretability of the history of the universe in human, spiritual terms; and the possibility of salvation through the contemplation of nature.

To Romantics, science must not bring about any split between nature and man. Romantics believed in the intrinsic ability of mankind to understand nature and its phenomena. They preferred not to dissect information as some insatiable thirst for knowledge and did not advocate what they viewed as the manipulation of nature, but rather mankind's acceptance of it.

Natural science, according to the Romantics, involved rejecting mechanical metaphors in favour of organic ones; in other words, they chose to view the world as composed of living beings with sentiments, rather than objects that merely function. Sir Humphry Davy, a prominent Romantic thinker, said that understanding nature required "an attitude of admiration, love and worship, a personal response." He believed that knowledge was only attainable by those who truly appreciated and respected nature. Self-understanding was an important aspect of Romanticism. It had less to do with proving that man was capable of understanding nature (through his budding intellect) and therefore controlling it, and more to do with the emotional appeal of connecting himself with nature and understanding it through a harmonious co-existence. Shelley's poem certainly sees humanity aspiring to a harmonious existence with the natural world. His consistent personification and the organic harmony he asserts is present in nature are also completely in tune with the Romantic view of the natural world and humanity – an organic, mutually-supportive relationship.

A Romantic Poem?

Let us be clear about one thing: this is NOT a Romantic poem because it is about love. It is, however, a Romantic poem because it deals with intimate, personal feelings and because (as we have just discussed above) it presents nature and humanity's relationship with it in a way that is in complete harmony with the Romantic view of nature and of science.

Shelley's 'Love's Philosophy':

- is a simple poem of persuasion;

- personifies nature throughout and links it to human behaviour;

- presents a view of nature and the natural world which has its roots in the Romantic view of science;

- uses simple language and repetition to present Shelley's ideas.

'Porphyria's Lover' – Robert Browning

Context

Robert Browning was born in 1812 and became one of the most famous English poets of the Victorian era. He was married to Elizabeth Barrett Browning who was a semi-invalid with an over-protective father. The couple were married in secret and then went to live in Italy. Browning's best work is often set in the past and he was a master of the dramatic monologue, in which the imagined speaker of the poem reveals their innermost thoughts and feelings, often going on to uncover uncomfortable truths about themselves.

porphyria – a rare disorder of the blood that may cause mental, nervous or skin problems.

vex – annoy, anger.

soiled – dirty, unclean.

dissever – to separate, to part in two.

oped – opened.

tress – a long lock of hair.

Who? The poem is a dramatic monologue spoken by the male lover of Porphyria.

When? One dark stormy might. Browning uses the weather as a pathetic fallacy for the turbulent human emotions in the cottage.

Where? In an isolated cottage.

What? The speaker, without a word of explanation or regret, tells of Porphyria's visit to him and his subsequent murder of her. The speaker spends the night alone with the body of his dead lover.

Commentary

'Porphyria's Lover' by Robert Browning dramatizes the conflicts between social pressures and romantic love; the tension between female submissiveness and the male urge to possess, to control and to act; the tension between momentary pleasure and the human need to preserve and keep that transitory pleasure; and the tension between strong religious faith and religious doubt.

In 'Porphyria's Lover' Browning presents a speaker who is insane. The poem was originally published in 1836 in the London journal *Monthly Repository* (Hawlin, 44) and was paired with another poem with an identical rhyme scheme, metre, line length and overall length (Ryals, 166). The paired poems were printed under the title 'Madhouse Cells' and the other poem, 'Johannes Agricola in Meditation', shares a similar preoccupation to 'Porphyria's Lover' – what Ryals calls the desire or will for 'total possession of another person' (166).

The poem is a dramatic monologue – a type of poem that Browning would continue to write throughout his career, but in this early example the monologue seems to be addressed to the reader; later dramatic monologues, such as 'My Last Duchess' and 'Fra Lippo Lippi' where Browning developed the form by including within the poem other characters to whom the monologue is addressed (Ryals, 87). In 'Porphyria's Lover' the speaker is isolated in many ways as we will see. The speaker is recounting the events of the previous evening, so the poem is written after the main event of the poem (which Browning, as the poet, cleverly delays until line 42.). The speaker – the lover of

Porphyria – has a tender tone as he recounts the events of the previous evening: indeed, Hawlin comments that his 'whole perspective is… gentle or feminized' (46). However, the speaker is also mad, and the crucial event of the poem in line 42, throws his previous solicitude and apparent love and care for Porphyria into a dark and deadly ironic light.

Browning's monologues are frequently voiced by eccentrics, lunatics, or people under emotional stress. Their ramblings illustrate character by describing the interactions of an odd personality with a particularly telling set of circumstances. In both 'Porphyria's Lover' and 'My Last Duchess', Browning uses this mode of exposition to describe a man who responds to the love of a beautiful woman by killing her. Each monologue offers the speakers' reasons for the desired woman from subject to object: in 'My Last Duchess', the Duke may have jealously murdered his wife, but keeps a portrait of her behind a curtain so none can look upon her smile without his permission; in 'Porphyria's Lover', the persona wishes to stop time at a single perfect moment and so kills his lover and sits all night embracing her carefully arranged body. It should be noted that in 'My Last Duchess' the woman's murder is at best implied, while in 'Porphyria's Lover' it is described quite explicitly by the speaker. The unchanging rhythmic pattern may also suggest the persona's insanity.

The 'Porphyria' persona's romantic egotism leads him into all manner of monstrously selfish assumptions compatible with his own longings. He seems convinced that Porphyria wanted to be murdered, and claims 'No pain felt she' while being strangled, adding, as if to convince himself, 'I am quite sure she felt no pain.' He may even believe she enjoyed the pain, because he, her lover, inflicted it. When she's dead, he says she's found her 'utmost will,' and when he sees her lifeless head drooping on his shoulder, he describes it as a 'smiling rosy little head', possibly using the word 'rosy' to symbolise the red roses of love, or to demonstrate his delusion that the girl, and their relationship, are still alive. More likely, however, is the thought that blood returning to her face, after the strangulation, makes her cheeks 'rosy.' Her 'rosy little head' may also be a sly reference to the hymen; Porphyria leaves a 'gay feast' and comes in from the outside world wearing 'soiled gloves'; now her blue eyes, open in death, are 'without a stain.' The lover may also be a fetishist, indicated by the fact that he refers to her hair numerous times throughout the poem, and strangles her with it. He also refers to the 'shut bud that holds a bee' which backs up the view of it being a sexual fetish.

It is impossible to know the true nature of his relationship to Porphyria. An incestuous relationship has been suggested; Porphyria might be the speaker's mother or sister. Another possibility is that she is a former lover, now betrothed, or even married, to some other man. Alternatively, they may be divided by social class.

Other sources speculate that the lover might be impotent, disabled, sick, or otherwise inadequate, and, as such, unable to satisfy Porphyria. There is much textual evidence to support this interpretation: he describes himself as 'one so pale / for love of her, and all in vain.' At the beginning of the poem, the persona never moves; he sits passively in a cold, dark room, sadly listening to the storm until Porphyria comes through 'wind and rain', 'shuts the cold out and the storm,' and makes up his dying fire. Finally, she sits beside him, calls his name, places his arm around her waist, and puts his head on her shoulder; interestingly, she has to stoop to do this. She is active; he is passive – suggesting impotence perhaps. At the poem's midpoint, the persona suddenly takes action, strangling Porphyria, propping her body against his, and boasting that afterwards, *her* head lay on *his* shoulder.

In line with the persona's suggested weakness and sickness, other scholars take the word 'porphyria' literally, and suggest that the seductress embodies a disease, and that the persona's killing of her is a sign of his recovery. Porphyria, which usually involved delusional madness and death, was classified several years before the poem's publication; Browning, who had an avid interest in such pathologies, may well have been aware of the new disease, and used it in this way to express his knowledge.

Much has been made of the final line: 'And yet, God has not said a word!' Possibly, the speaker seeks divine approval for the murder. He may believe God has said nothing because He is satisfied with his actions. God may be satisfied because: He recognises that the persona's crime is the only way to keep Porphyria pure; or, because He doesn't think her life and death are important compared to the persona's. The persona may also be waiting in vain for some sign of God's approval. Alternatively, the line may represent his feelings of emptiness in the wake of his violence; Porphyria is gone, quiet descends, and he's alone. The persona may also be **schizophrenic**; he may be listening for a voice in his head, which he mistakes for the voice of God. It has also been postulated that this is Browning's statement of 'God's silence,' in which neither good nor bad acts are immediately recompensed by the deity.

The final line may also register the persona's sense of guilt over his crime. Despite his elaborate justifications for his act, he has, in fact, committed murder, and he expects God to punish him – or, at least, to take notice. The persona is surprised, perhaps a little uneasy, at God's continued silence. An alternative reading of the last line is to identify a slightly gleeful tone in it – confirming once again that the speaker is insane.

There is no doubt of his insanity; exactly why he kills Porphyria is open to debate and interpretation.

The poem is set in an isolated rural cottage: Browning implies this because Porphyria who has walked through a storm to meet her lover is completely wet and immediately takes off her 'dripping cloak and shawl' (line 11) and her 'soiled gloves' (line 12). Browning uses the storm as a pathetic fallacy in at least three ways: firstly, it is an effective contrast with the warmth and love within the cottage once Porphyria lights the fire and makes advances to her lover; secondly, it can be seen as Browning foreshadowing the later, violent events of the poem; and, thirdly, it might even be seen as symbolizing the tortured inner feelings of Porphyria's 'murderously jealous lover' (Hair & Kennedy, 88) – feelings which he keeps under careful control. Knoepflmacher argues that Browning presents very well the 'contrast between a cold outside world and a warm interior' (158) and Porphyria herself can be seen as 'the passionate outsider penetrating that interior who brings warmth to the immobile dreamer within' (158). However, this can be seen as an example of prolepsis, since, despite the speaker's self-delusional assertions, in death Porphyria's body will rapidly lose all its warmth.

The relationship between the two lovers is presented by Browning as a clandestine one, but one which Porphyria wants: she has, after all, braved a storm to visit her lover and the way she 'put my arm about her waist,/And made her smooth white shoulder bare' (lines 16 -17) clearly suggests that the relationship is sexual. It seems that Browning suggests that it has to be clandestine because Porphyria and her lover are from different classes: Martens asserts that the poem is essentially about a man's 'pathological love for a socially-superior woman' (39). Browning suggests this through the speaker's words: he says that Porphyria is 'too weak... from pride' (lines 22 & 24) – presumably a pride issuing from her social superiority and the disgrace she would suffer if her love for this man became known, and he goes on to say that she is 'too weak' (line 22) to allow her 'struggling passion free' (line 23) and 'give herself to me forever' (line 25), because she is socially bound by what the speaker dismisses as 'vainer ties' (line 24) – presumably her sense of responsibility to her family. Browning presents the speaker as being very distraught at this situation: it explains why he does not respond in line 15 when she calls him and he comments that, because he cannot have her forever or is dependent on her secret visits to him, it seems that his love for her is 'all in vain' (line 30). But passion prevails – Browning hints perhaps that they make love and, as they do so, the man notices how Porphyria is looking at him and realizes 'I knew/Porphyria worshipped me' (lines 33 -34). He goes on:' That moment she was mine, mine, fair,/Perfectly pure and good' (line 38). But it is only a moment of intense feeling and, given what Browning has suggested about the nature of their relationship and his dependence on her coming to him when she can and not when she or he both want, he decides to preserve the moment and strangles her with her own hair. The repeated 'mine, mine' in line 37 convey his extreme possessiveness and Knoepflmacher writes that 'by draining Porphyria of her life, he can assume… control' (160). This can easily be seen as symptomatic of the masculine desire to possess and control, the human desire to preserve forever a moment of happiness, and we might even see the speaker as rebelling against a rigid class system which keeps him and his lover apart. However, by killing Porphyria, Browning presents the insane speaker as having wholly abrogated all moral responsibility for his actions and acted in defiance of human law and morality.

Mirroring the speaker's desire for control, the poem's structure is highly controlled. On the page the poem looks highly regular and it is: Browning conveys his speaker's thoughts with a regular unvarying rhyme scheme which consists of units of six lines which rhyme ABABB, CDCDD and so on. This tightly-controlled and very regular rhyme scheme could be said to mirror the speaker's own need for control and his obsession with Porphyria; at the same time, despite the horrific nature of his crime, his speaking voice remains calm and untroubled – just as the poem is very formally and regularly structured. Hawlin (42) describes the rhyme scheme as 'assymetrical' – presumably meaning that we might expect the six line unit to rhyme like this – ABABAB – but the rhyme scheme that Browning has chosen with the fifth and sixth line rhyming with each other, means that in terms of rhyme, the six line unit turns back on itself – an attempt surely to accentuate the self-obsessed, inward-looking nature of the speaker. In other words, the speaker is concerned only with his own feelings, despite his apparent concern for Porphyria – (No pain felt she;/I am quite sure she felt no pain' (lines 42 – 43). As Bailey asserts, the speaker has a 'megalomaniac stance towards his lover' (53), and he is 'self-deceiving' (Hair & Kennedy, 88). This self-deception and the evidence of his insanity continues after Porphyria is dead: the speaker thinks that her eyes 'laughed… without a stain' (line 46) and that 'her cheek once more/Blushed bright beneath my burning kiss' (lines 48 -49).

Browning uses a lot of enjambment – twenty-two times in a poem of sixty lines - so that over a third of the lines run on and are not end-stopped. On the one hand, it could be said that this enjambment helps convey the impression of a real voice that is speaking, but there is perhaps another purpose: in so many lines the words and syntax break through the end of the line and this is a poem about a speaker who breaks accepted morality by committing murder. Furthermore, the lines which build up to and describe Porphyria's murder – lines 32 to 42 – use an excessive amount of enjambment which perhaps help to convey the speaker's frenzy, emphasize his breaking of the rules and quicken the rhythm of the poem to its climax, as well as imitating the speedy act of strangling his lover. Browning's use of heavy, full-stop caesuras is equally significant. He uses only two: one in line 15 after Prophyria 'sat down by my side/And called me.' (lines 14 – 15) – a caesura which is used to emphasize the speaker's lack of response to her; the second in line 42 after 'strangled her' – which again serves, for the reader, to emphasize the enormity of the crime he has committed. The caesura helps to foreground the act of murder. However, Browning presents the speaker as so delusional that he argues that in killing his lover he was doing what she would have wanted: he describes her head as 'so glad it has its utmost will' (line 54) and he claims in his insanity that his killing of her is 'her darling one wish' (line 58). The speaker's final observation – that on the subject of the murder 'God has not said a word!' (line 60) – certainly shows the speaker's contempt and insouciance towards religious diktats forbidding murder.

Browning's 'Porphyria's Lover' is a deeply disturbing poem, enhanced by the strict regularity of the rhyme scheme and the control that Browning exerts over it. What appears to be a passionate story of the secret tryst of two lovers turns into a tale of sudden and violent murder, and a crazed and deluded justification of it. Ryals states that 'there has been some disagreement as to whether the lover kills Porphyria because he loves her or hates her' (271): it could be argued that such a question is irrelevant because, love her or hate her, he seeks to possess her completely and forever. It can be seen that the poem raises other issues – the unfairness of the British class system, the habitual, historical male need to dominate and a growing scepticism about God – but these are overshadowed by the pathological and wholly solipsistic megalomania of the speaker.

Works Cited

Bailey, Suzanne. *Cognitive Style and Perceptual Difference in Browning's Poetry*. London: Routledge, 2010. Print.

Browning, Robert. 'Porphyria's Lover'. *Poetry Foundation*. Web. October 28th, 2013.

Hair, Donald S. & Kennedy, Richard S. *The Dramatic Imagination of Robert Browning: A Literary Life*. Columbia, Mi: University of Missouri Press, 2007. Print.

Hawlin, Stefan. *Robert Browning*. London: Routledge, 2012. Print.

Knoepflmacher, U. C. 'Projection of the Female Other: Romanticism, Browning and the Victorian Dramatic Monologue'. Pp. 147 – 168 in Claridge, Laura & Langland, Elizabeth (eds.). *Out of Bounds: Male Writers and Gendered Criticism*. Boston, Ma: University of Massachusetts Press, 1990. Print.

Martens, Britta. *Browning, Victorian Poetics and the Romantic Legacy: Challenging the Personal Voice*. London: Aldgate Publishing Ltd, 2011. Print.

Ryals, Clyde de L. *Robert Browning: The Poems and Plays of Robert Browning, 1833 – 1846*. Columbus, Oh: Ohio State University Press, 1983. Print.

In 'Porphyria's Lover' Browning:

- uses dramatic monologue to present a solipsistic, psychopathic maniac;

- to suggest an illicit love affair, perhaps caused by social differences;

- uses a rigid rhyme scheme and metre to suggest the speaker's confidence and rigidity of thinking, but also uses caesura brilliantly at key moments;

- presents an insane mind obsessed with full possession of his lover;

- in the poem presents possessive love as a life-denying force.

Further Reading

What follows is the poem that was paired with 'Porphyria's Lover' by Browning under the title 'Madhouse Cells': it is very different from 'Porphyria's Lover', but is worth reading because it shows Browning presenting another character who suffers from extreme solipsism and a psychopathic conviction that he is right. It is another portrait of an insane character.

'Johannes Agricola in Meditation' (1836)

The speaker believes in an extreme form of predestination, claiming that, since he's one of the elect, he can commit any sin without forfeiting his afterlife in heaven.

There's heaven above, and night by night
I look right through its gorgeous roof;
No suns and moons though e'er so bright
Avail to stop me; splendour-proof
I keep the broods of stars aloof:
For I intend to get to God,
For 't is to God I speed so fast,
For in God's breast, my own abode,
Those shoals of dazzling glory, passed,
I lay my spirit down at last.
I lie where I have always lain,
God smiles as he has always smiled;

Ere suns and moons could wax and wane,
Ere stars were thundergirt, or piled
The heavens, God thought on me his child;
Ordained a life for me, arrayed
Its circumstances every one
To the minutest; ay, God said
This head this hand should rest upon
Thus, ere he fashioned star or sun.
And having thus created me,
Thus rooted me, he bade me grow,
Guiltless for ever, like a tree
That buds and blooms, nor seeks to know
The law by which it prospers so:
But sure that thought and word and deed
All go to swell his love for me,
Me, made because that love had need
Of something irreversibly
Pledged solely its content to be.
Yes, yes, a tree which much ascend,
No poison-gourd foredoomed to stoop!
I have God's warrant, could I blend
All hideous sins, as in a cup,
To drink the mingled venoms up;
Secure my nature will convert
The draught to blossoming gladness fast:
While sweet dews turn to the gourd's hurt,
And bloat, and while they bloat it, blast,
As from the first its lot was cast.
For as I lie, smiled on, full-fed
By unexhausted power to bless,
I gaze below on hell's fierce bed,
And those its waves of flame oppress,
Swarming in ghastly wretchedness;
Whose life on earth aspired to be
One altar-smoke, so pure! -- to win
If not love like God's love for me,
At least to keep his anger in;
And all their striving turned to sin.
Priest, doctor, hermit, monk grown white

With prayer, the broken-hearted nun,
The martyr, the wan acolyte,
The incense-swinging child, -- undone
Before God fashioned star or sun!
God, whom I praise; how could I praise,
If such as I might understand,
Make out and reckon on his ways,
And bargain for his love, and stand,
Paying a price at his right hand?'

'Sonnet XXIX' – Elizabeth Barrett Browning

Context

Elizabeth Barrett Browning was born into a wealthy family in 1806. At the age of 14 she suffered from a lung complaint and the following year damaged her spine in a riding accident; she was to be plagued with poor health for the rest of her life. Elizabeth had started to publish poetry anonymously and was starting to become famous. In 1838 her brother Edward drowned off the coast of Devon and for the next five years Elizabeth became a recluse, hardly leaving her bedroom in her father's house. However, she continued to write poetry and began a long correspondence with the poet Robert Browning, who began writing to her after reading her poems. Between 1844 and 1846 they wrote 574 letters to each other and finally ran away to Italy to get married. They had to flee to Italy because Elizabeth's father was violently opposed to the marriage. She and her father never spoke again and he disinherited her. Her health improved in Italy and she gave birth to a son in 1849. She died in her husband's arms in 1861.

'Sonnet XXIX' is from the sonnet cycle *Sonnets from the Portuguese* which she wrote during their correspondence and before their marriage. (*Sonnets from the Portuguese* is simply the title she chose – they are not translations and do not exist in Portuguese!). This sonnet cycle explores the development and growth of her love for Browning and, although she wrote many other poems, it is these sonnets for which she is mainly remembered today. What is interesting and rarely mentioned in guides like this, is that the earlier poems in the sonnet cycle were not as confident as 'Sonnet'. In the earlier sonnets she is afraid of the consequences of her love for Browning and unsure about her own feelings: 'Sonnet XXIX' is from the middle of the sonnet cycle and represents the achievement of a confident, mature love.

insphere – to encircle or surround

Who? The sonnet was written by Elizabeth Barrett Browning before she was married to Robert Browning. The poem is addressed to her future husband.

When? The poem was published in 1850 as part of a 44 sonnet cycle entitled 'Sonnets from the Portuguese'. Despite the title they are completely original and not based on any Portuguese poems at all. Within the poem there is no specific time.

Where? No specific location.

What? This is a highly personal poem and Barrett Browning describes her thoughts and feelings when she is not with her lover.

Commentary

The opening exclamation, emphasized by the heavy caesura, conveys Barrett Browning's excitement when she thinks about her lover and future husband. The enjambment between lines one and two and again between lines three and four add to the air of sheer excitement that she feels. The opening quatrain also introduces the central metaphor which runs throughout the poem: her lover is a tree and Barrett Browning's thoughts are like 'wild vines' that 'twine and bud' around the tree. This is an interesting metaphor: the word 'wild' suggests her passion and excitement, while the image of her lover as a tree suggests something strong, upright and dependable; the vines only exist because they can twine around the tree, suggesting that Barrett Browning is nothing without her lover. The tree also is clearly a phallic image, emphasizing her lover's masculinity. The central metaphor – because it is drawn from nature – also suggests that their love is natural as well as exciting and passionate. In line 3 she orders him to 'put out broad leaves', so that the trunk of the tree cannot be seen when the broad leaves mingle with her 'wild vines'. Again his strength is contrasted to her relative weakness: her vines (which use the tree as a support) are merely the 'straggling green'.

The second quatrain begins with a direct address to her lover – 'Yet, O my palm tree' – which continues the metaphor and with 'yet' suggests she is going to raise a contradiction to the opening quatrain. In lines 5, 6 and 7 she explains that having thoughts about him is a feeble substitute for actually being with him and the lines gain intensity from the enjambment which suggests impatience and passion at the same time. In line 7 she exclaims that he is 'dearer, better!' – and this is given added force by the strong caesura of the exclamation mark. She orders him with a series of imperatives:

Renew thy presence; as a strong tree should,

Rustle thy boughs and set thy trunk all bare

Barrett Browning does not have a traditional volta or turn in line 9 of this sonnet, but the long sentence which starts on line 7 changes the course of the thought and feeling in the sonnet. She wants all the 'bands of greenery' which 'insphere' him to 'drop heavily down' – so that there are no barriers between them. She uses images of violence and an exclamation to suggest the strength of her desire to see him and be with him: the greenery will be 'burst, shattered, everywhere!' The image of 'thy trunk all bare' has strong phallic overtones.

And why does she want all the greenery to be stripped away so that it drops 'heavily down'?

Because, in this deep joy to see and hear thee

And breathe within thy shadow a new air,

I do not think of thee – I am too near thee.

When they are together or when they will be together, she has no need to think of him as she is overwhelmed by his physical presence. The poem began with 'I think of thee', but ends with 'I do not think of thee' – an interesting reversal of words, caused by their finally being together.

Barrett Browning's father's opposition to her marriage to Robert Browning is important to remember. It was unusual in the early Victorian period for middle class women to defy their fathers as Barrett Browning did. Some readers have seen in the imagery of the greenery being 'burst' and 'shattered', the hope that they can be together and defy the wishes of her father. The image of breaking free from the 'vines' could be seen as a reference to the speaker breaking free from her father's domination. Barrett Browning's excitement, commitment and passion for her lover are clear throughout the sonnet.

Elizabeth Barrett Browning's 'Sonnet XXIX':

- is a fiercely passionate and excited poem about Barrett Browning's love for Robert Browning with strong sexual connotations;

- it follows the form of a Petrarchan sonnet with two quatrains and a sestet, but the speaker's exclamations and frequent use of enjambment convey her passion and excitement;

- uses an extended metaphor with Robert Browning as a solid, strong tree and Elizabeth as the leaves and vines that grow up the trunk of the tree;

- the metaphor has been 'shattered' in line 11 because thinking about him is a poor substitute for being with him – and the last three lines imagine their successful meeting and perhaps the consummation of their love. She has no need to think of him or to construct elaborate metaphors about their love, because they are together.

'Neutral Tones' – Thomas Hardy

Context

Thomas Hardy (1840 – 1928) is best known as a novelist. He wrote 15 novels, most of which are set largely in Dorset and the surrounding counties, and which deal with the ordinary lives of ordinary people in stories in which they struggle to find happiness and love – often battling against fate or their own circumstances. His final two novels *Tess of the D'Urbervilles* (1891) and *Jude the Obscure* (1895) both portray sex outside marriage in a sympathetic way and there was such a hysterical public outcry about the novels that Hardy stopped writing fiction and devoted the rest of his life to poetry. Although much of his poetry reflects his interest in nature and ordinary things, this poem is also typical of his work in that it is intensely personal and may reflect the intense unhappiness he felt in his first marriage.

Neutral – this can refer to the landscape, drained of vivid colours, but can also refer to the lovers in the poem – who are presented as being completely indifferent to one another.

Tones – like 'neutral' above this can refer to colour (or the lack of it), but also to the mood of the former lovers.

chidden – this is the past of 'to chide'. To chide means to tell off or to reprimand. Here it is as though God had told off the white sun.

sod – turf, the earth with grass on it.

rove – wander.

bird-a-wing – a bird in flight.

curst - cursed

Who? There is no reason to assume that the speaker is not Hardy himself. His lover is with him in the poem and this is seen in Hardy's use of the third person plural – 'we'.

When? On a cold winter's day. Hardy wrote the poem in 1867 at the age of 27, but it was not published until 1898.

Where? In the countryside beside a pond.

What? Hardy is looking back with bitterness and intense sadness at the end of a relationship.

Commentary

This is a bitter and pessimistic poem about the break-up of a relationship – one which Hardy remembers vividly and which still causes him pain and anguish. As a 'break up' poem, it is hard to think of a better one in the English Language – unless it's Byron's 'When We Two Parted'. Hardy uses pathetic fallacy throughout the poem, so the details of the weather and the landscape match and mirror the emotions of the two lovers.

The first stanza sets the scene. It is a bleak winter's day and the speaker and his former lover are standing by a pond. The landscape seems stripped of all fertility and strength. There are a few grey ash leaves scattered about and the sun, source of heat and light and life, is 'white, as though chidden of God' – chidden for being 'white' and for not offering any heat or real light on this miserable day? The sod is starving just as this relationship is starved now of any real love or affection.

In the second stanza Hardy directly addresses his lover, the first line using parallelism – 'eyes on me/eyes that rove'. Her eyes are like eyes that wander over 'tedious riddles of years ago' – suggesting that the relationship has been going on for years but that it has become 'tedious' – monotonous and uninteresting – a long time ago. They exchange some words (which Hardy does not bother to use in the poem) and he writes that the words they exchange – 'lost the more by our love': the words they speak now are trivial and meaningless and are in contrast to the love they once felt for each other. They are dull and irrelevant now (lost the more) in comparison with the love they once enjoyed (our love).

Hardy begins the third stanza with a scathing and oxymoronic simile by writing:

The smile on your mouth was the deadest thing

Alive enough to have strength to die –

which stresses the winter sterility of nature around them, but also accuses his lover of hypocrisy – why should she be smiling given the state of their relationship? Is it for form's sake or to try and keep up the pretence that they still mean something to each other? But then his lover makes 'a grin of bitterness' which is compared to 'an ominous bird-a-wing'. Some readers of Hardy have made the point that in his poems he uses birds in an ominous and usually pessimistic way – which is only interesting because it contrasts so sharply with the Romantic poets' use of birds in their poems. The Romantics (who preceded Hardy) almost always use birds as symbols of hope, poetic inspiration or the uplifting power of nature. Hardy – it could be argued – is more modern in his sensibility using birds as symbols of something negative and life-denying.

Hardy in the final stanza is writing from an imagined present and writes:

Since then, keen lessons that love deceives,

And wrings with wrong, have shaped to me

Your face, and the God-curst sun, and a tree

And a pond edged with grayish leaves.

'Since then' suggests the incident is long ago. Hardy suggests that he has been in love since then, but without success: he has learnt 'keen lessons' that 'love deceives', and whenever he does his mind thinks back to this unsuccessful meeting by the pond. The alliteration of 'wrings with wrong' sounds unpleasant and the venom (partly in the sound, partly in the meaning) of 'God-curst sun' is very bleak and powerful. In artistic terms Hardy brings the poem full circle to end where he began – the pond, the tree, the gray leaves. The pond is stagnant like the relationship, and is part of the pathetic fallacy used through the poem – the dead leaves, the white sun. The landscape is drained of all colour – just as the relationship is drained of all love.

Byron's 'When We Two Parted' is clearly about one individual woman. Hardy's poem is based on a meeting with one individual woman, but he has learnt 'keen lessons that love deceives' since then, which suggests a series of unsuccessful relationships, with the one in 'Neutral Tones' being the first of many. And in what ways can love deceive? Our first thought might be infidelity, but that is not very subtle. Hardy might mean pretending to yourself that you love someone or falling in love with someone before discovering what they are really like or just falling in love with the wrong person. I'm sure you can think of other possibilities. Hardy is claiming that at the end of any relationship he thinks back to this scene by the pond because of its sterile desolation: perhaps it was also the end of his first serious love affair.

Hardy chooses to use a regular rhyme scheme and the poem is made up of four rhyming quatrains written in iambic tetrameter – eight syllables to the line with four stressed syllables. However, Hardy uses enjambment skillfully and there is some metrical variation: 'God-curst sun' consists of three stressed syllables which adds force and power to the words themselves.

In 'Neutral Tones' Hardy

- writes a devastatingly bleak poem about the end of a relationship;

- uses pathetic fallacy in a masterly way to convey the human emotions in the poem;

- writes with a sense of experience about the bitter feelings that relationships can cause;

- apportions no blame for the breakdown of the relationship;

- uses imagery well to convey the sterility of the landscape and by extension the sterility of the relationship.

'The Farmer's Bride' – Charlotte Mew

Context

Charlotte Mew was born in London in 1869. Her father died in 1898, leaving his family in poverty. Three of her siblings died in childhood and another two suffered from mental illness and were put in hospital permanently. Charlotte and her remaining sister, Anne, made a pact never to marry for fear of passing on insanity to their children. She started publishing short stories in 1896, but her first collection of poetry (for which this poem provided the title) was not published until 1916. After the death of Anne, she descended into a deep depression and eventually committed suicide in 1928.

maid – young girl – the implication is also that she is a virgin

bide – wait

woo – a slightly old-fashioned word now, it means to court or win the affections of someone.

fay – a fairy.

fall – autumn. We associate this word with American English, but there is evidence that it survived as a term for *autumn* in some regions of the UK until at least 1900.

abed – in bed

fast – tightly locked

beseech – to ask or pray earnestly.

leveret – a young hare; more technically, a hare that is less than a year old.

betwixt – between.

Who? The poet speaks as a farmer who has married a young girl who is scared of men and sex. He tells us a lot about his wife. He also has neighbours who help catch his wife when she runs off.

When? The farmer speaks in the past tense before switching to the present in the third stanza.

Where? It is set in a rural community on a farm and there is a closeness to the natural world and the rhythms and seasons of nature expressed through the imagery.

What? The farmer describes what has happened in his life since he got married just over a year before the poem starts.

Commentary

This poem's narrator is a farmer who tells the story of his courtship of his wife and the progress of their three year marriage.

In the first stanza we are told that on reflection he thinks that perhaps she was too young. He married her quickly in the summer of one year because it was harvest time and he had more pressing things to attend to – bringing in the harvest. The marriage has not gone well. We are not told exactly why, but husband and wife do not sleep together and the final line of the opening stanza tells us that the wife tried to run away, because she was so repulsed by her husband and, it is suggested, having sex with her husband. As soon as they were married we are told

... she turned afraid

Of love and me and all things human.

And then *her smile went out* and one night in the autumn she simply ran away.

In the second stanza the husband recounts how he and others from the community chased her in the dark, found her, brought her home and locked her up. She was among the sheep, he was told, but she wasn't and so *we chased her*. It is not clear who *we* are – the farmer and his friends or his neighbours or other members of the community perhaps; what is important, I think, is that it was a group of people chasing after one frightened young woman. They finally caught up with her at Church-town. She was

All in a shiver and a scare

but they ignore her fear, take her home and lock her in the farmer's house. Line 13 is an interesting line. The farmer says she should have been in bed:

Lying awake with her wide brown stare.

We go to bed to sleep, but this line suggests that normally she does not sleep: this suggests that she deliberately stays awake in order not to be taken sexually in her sleep.

In the third stanza the tense changes to describe the present state of affairs. She performs the work about the house and is happy in the company of small creatures

With birds and rabbits and such as they,

but she becomes disturbed whenever any man comes near her. She doesn't say anything but the eyes beseech them not to come near her. The women around the farm have noticed that she seems to have an especial affinity with animals when she speaks to them. The farmer ruefully comments in the final line of the stanza that

I've never heard her speak at all.

The speaker changes tone in the fifth stanza which runs from line 30 to line 41. The first four lines describe his wife in a sympathetic way and in a series of similes all drawn from nature. The sibilance creates a wistful sense of longing - the narrator is clearly attracted to his wife. Line 34 switches to describe the autumn in loving yet elegiac tones: the year is ending, the days are getting shorter, the leaves are falling – there is a sense of nature dying off, all the more beautiful because Mew uses almost wholly monosyllabic words for the rest of the stanza. But in line 39 the narrator mentions the berries on the holly trees getting redder and this reminds him that it will soon be Christmas. The red berries have a symbolic function: red is associated with passion: when a woman's virginity is taken and her hymen broken she often sheds blood: here though the symbol is ironic because sex has not occurred between the farmer and his bride. The stanza ends with the farmer wishing that he had children so that Christmas would be more fulfilling.

What's Christmas-time without there be

Some other in the house than we!

It is one of the central ironies of this poem that farmers produce food which keeps us alive, but this farmer cannot produce children because his wife will not sleep with him.

In the final stanza the voice of the farmer breaks down and, to reflect this, the pattern of the stanza changes and is much shorter and, therefore, more intense. The farmer seems wracked with sexual frustration. His wife sleeps on the floor above him in the attic. So she is physically quite close to him, but not in the same bed. He could reach her very easily, but knows he would frighten her and that she does not want him. Are we to imagine that the attic door is locked? I think we are – or she would run away as she has done before. As he thinks of her he is overwhelmed with physical desire for her youthful skin and the beauty of her eyes and hair. The final sentence begins with an exclamation and then becomes very repetitive as the farmer expresses his almost uncontrolled longing for her. The repetition and the internal rhyme here accentuate his torment and the unfulfilled passion for her:

... Oh! My God! The down,

The soft young down of her, the brown,

The brown of her – her eyes, her hair, her hair!

Down is an interesting word to use because it means and is associated with animals. Throughout the poem the wife has been associated with nature or with things that are not human: *fay, like a hare, like a mouse, a leveret, a young larch tree, the first wild violets*. Furthermore, she has an affinity with animals. Farmers control nature, but the wife is compared or associated with things that we cannot control.

Mew is very successful in creating the voice of the farmer. The vocabulary she uses is very simple and the imagery is drawn from the natural world – the world which the farmer would know so well. There are phrases which suggest a man of little formal education and a slightly old-fashioned or ungrammatical way of expressing himself all through the poem, such as *more's to do, the shut of a winter's day, 'twasn't a woman, runned, her be, fetched her home, men-folk, betwixt*. It is a remarkable feat of ventriloquism. Like other dramatic monologues the speaker reveals more and more of himself as the poem proceeds.

This poem could be read as a simple story of male oppression. After all, the wife tries to run away and now cannot because she is locked in the attic. Her imprisonment here recalls the fate of other fictional heroines such as Mr Rochester's wife in *Jane Eyre* and the central character in *The Yellow Wallpaper* by Charlotte Perkins Gilman. Her association with animals and other natural things might suggest that the farmer is trying to control something natural and force it to do his will; but this imagery is paradoxically the very reason why he finds her so attractive – because she reminds him of the animals he is surrounded by in nature.

However, Mew presents the farmer as essentially sympathetic. He uses his power over her, but he controls his sexual desire for his wife and recognizes that she does not want him. Marital rape was not recognized as a crime in the UK until 1991. In the period that Mew was writing in, it would have been considered normal for the husband to have forced himself onto his wife – it would certainly not have been illegal. But the farmer is perceptive enough to know that she fears him and a sexual relationship. And, although he locks her up, he is, in the context of the times, in control of his urges and sympathetic to her lack of desire for him. His descriptions of her – especially those which compare her to small animals – could be said to display a certain amount of patience towards her – even sympathy or empathy. Equally you could say that these descriptions are slightly condescending and patronizing, because they do not individualize her or see her humanity. We are never told her name and the title of the poem could be said to sum her up: from the farmer's point of view, her only role in life is to be his bride and give him sex and children.

He is not especially cruel to her, but he is rather conventional. He has married in order to have children, perhaps so that they can inherit the farm. He expects her to have sex with him and is filled with frustration that she does not want to. She seems to like animals because, you could argue, she is treated like one: the beasts are kept in their stalls; she is kept in her attic. In addition, we might note that she has a natural affinity which the women have noticed, with small frightened creatures like herself.

Why?

This dramatic monologue

- presents two people trapped in a marriage;

- the wife is literally held prisoner in her husband's house;

- the husband is full of desire for his wife, but sensitive enough to ignore his physical desires;

- examines the imprisoning role that women had to fulfill in the past;

- describes nature in beautiful colloquial language especially in lines 34 to 39;

- shows two people who are both in different ways in tune with nature;

- is full of the wife's fear and the husband's unrequited desires – which can never be reconciled.

'Walking Away' – C Day Lewis

Context

This poem was first published in 1962 in the collection 'The Gate and Other Poems'. It is dedicated to Day-Lewis's first son, Sean, and recalls a day when he was watching Sean go into school. It has become one of his most enduring works and in 2001 was chosen by readers of the *Radio Times* as one of their top ten poems of childhood.

leaves just turning – it is the start of Autumn and the leaves are just turning colour from green to brown and red.

like a satellite – when the poem was written space exploration was in its infancy and satellites were very new, modern things.

pathos – the quality that produces pity.

half-fledged – a fully fledged bird is able to fly, so it follows that Day Lewis's son is not yet capable of independent flight.

gait – manner of walking.

a winged seed – sycamore trees have winged seeds.

irresolute – weak in purpose.

clay – the human body; it has acquired this meaning because in the Christian Bible God makes man from clay.

selfhood – a sense of oneself as a unique individual.

Who? The poet is the speaker of the poem. He is watching his son walk away from him at the end of his first football match, surrounded by the other players. The poem is addressed to his son.

When? The poem was first published in 1962, but is about a memory from 18 years before.

Where? On a school playing field.

What? The poem deals with the son growing up and leaving his close parental bond behind him as he sets out to live his own life. At the end of the poem the tone is one of sadness at this inevitable process and an acceptance too that one's children, one day, have to walk away to their own lives.

Commentary

The first stanza is full of one particular memory. Day Lewis remembers that it is eighteen years since he watched his son play his first football match. The experience has been powerful enough to stay with him and the details – 'the leaves just turning', 'a sunny day' and 'the touch-lines new ruled' – give the memory its vivid quality as does the poet's use of the present tense. At the end of the game Day Lewis watches his son

like a satellite

Wrenched from its orbit, go drifting away...

The word 'away' occurs somewhere in each stanza and three times at the end of a line, emphasizing his son's movement away from him as he grows older. He watches his son walk away from him towards the school

With the pathos of a half-fledged thing set free

Into a wilderness, the gait of one

Who finds no path where the path should be.

He obviously feels his son is not ready for complete freedom yet even though he has started on that path. His plight causes the poet to feel pathos for his son who has been set free but has no path to follow.

This sense of aimless, uninformed movement informs the simile at the opening of the third stanza: his son is a 'hesitant figure' – 'like a winged seed loosed from its parent stem'. This leads Day Lewis to admit that he never manages (either in life or in writing perhaps) to convey

About nature's give and take – the small, the scorching

Ordeals which fire one's irresolute clay.

This looks tricky to understand, but is not really. Nature gives and takes – he is given a son but the son will leave and have an independent life. This causes pain – 'the small, scorching ordeals' – even the tiny ordeal of watching his son walk away from him at the end of a football match. 'Clay' is being used here to mean our personality; however, clay is also used to make vases and plates and it is fixed in position by being 'fired' – heated at very strong temperatures. And so our personalities are fired (created) by our experiences. Watching his son walk away from him causes Day Lewis pain and is a 'small, scorching ordeal' – perhaps one of innumerable ones that Day Lewis feels but which add to his personality.

Despite the football match being eighteen years ago. Day Lewis is haunted by it still:

I have had worse partings, but none that so

Gnaws at my mind still.

Day Lewis suggests tentatively ('perhaps') the sadness he feels at watching his son walk away shows

How selfhood begins with a walking away,

And love is proved in the letting go.

In other words, his son must 'walk away' to become a fully-grown, independent adult and that, because that process is inevitable, true parental love will let go of the child and encourage the child on the road to selfhood.

The readers of the *Radio Times* may have voted this their favourite poem of childhood, but I feel it reveals more about the adult poet and his sadness and regret that his son must 'walk away' and grow up. A parent's natural desire to protect their children from the world and to preserve their innocence is doomed to failure, and the poem is more about Day Lewis's feelings than his son's. The poet's mention of the 'small, scorching ordeals' of everyday life suggest he is sensitive and aware of how the tiniest actions or events in life can trigger strong emotions. This is a poem about how adults cope with seeing their children grow up.

The poem is written in four stanzas of five lines each with the first, the third and the fifth lines rhyming, which suggests that the poet has his feelings under control after years of reflection on the incident. However, only three of the lines are end-stopped and the enjambment suggests the continued strength and distress of his feelings. He feels great pain for what he sees as his son's vulnerability, and the fact that as a parent he can do nothing to stop a process that is inevitable for all children. The final line of the poem brings closure to the angst that the poet feels: 'love is proved in the letting go'.

Overall, despite the hard-won stoicism of the last line, the poem is generally sad and regretful. Its popularity may be due to its relative simplicity – the son's simple act of walking off a football pitch with the other players becoming symbolic of something much larger and universal in its scope. The two similes – the satellite and the spinning tree seed – are easy to relate to, and any reader who has children will identify with the basic premise of the poem – that it is hard to let go of one's children.

In C Day Lewis's 'Walking Away':

- the poet writes movingly about the ordeal and pain that every parent feels as their children grow up;

- comes to an acceptance – memorably expressed in the final line - that the process of growing up is inevitable and that a parent's true love is shown by letting go;

- uses a regular stanza and rhyme scheme but lots of enjambment to show the strength of his feelings;

- uses straightforward language and simple similes to communicate deep and personal feelings.

'Letters from Yorkshire' – Maura Dooley

Context

Maura Dooley was born in Truro, grew up in Bristol, and, after working for some years in Yorkshire, now lives in London. She is a freelance writer and lectures at Goldsmiths' College. She edited *Making for Planet Alice: New Women Poets* (1997) and *The Honey Gatherers: A Book of Love Poems* (2002) for Bloodaxe, and *How Novelists Work* (2000) for Seren. *Life Under Water* (Bloodaxe Books, 2008) is her first new collection since *Sound Barrier: Poems 1982-2002* (Bloodaxe Books, 2002), since then her others include *Explaining Magnetism* (1991) and *Kissing a Bone* (1996), both Poetry Book Society Recommendations. *Kissing a Bone* was shortlisted for the T.S. Eliot Prize and *Life Under Water* has been shortlisted for the T. S. Eliot Prize 2008. This poem was first published in 2002 in a collection called *Sound Barrier*.

Who? The poet writes as herself and about an unidentified 'you' who lives in Yorkshire and is male. The first stanza begins with third person narration, but swiftly changes to direct address of 'you'. By the final stanza Dooley is using the third person plural – 'our'.

When? The poem was published in 2002 in a collection called *Sound Barrier*. It has a contemporary setting.

Where? The poem is addressed to someone living in Yorkshire, while the poet lives in the city (presumably London).

What? The poem juxtaposes the two very different life styles that the poet and the person living in Yorkshire lead, but celebrates the fact that they keep in touch.

Commentary

This poem is about a long-distance relationship conducted by letters – quite an old-fashioned form of communication in the early 21st century. The speaker of the poem lives and works in London (or another big city) as a journalist; the other person lives in Yorkshire in a rural environment and the poem presents these two contrasting lifestyles very vividly. The relationship is one of simple friendship: the speaker asserts in the second stanza – 'It's not romance', simply friendship. In fact, the nature of the relationship is never made clear: the poet is female and appears to be talking as herself, while her friend is male but clearly not a relative.

The first stanza uses the third person – he' – and the past tense. Dooley uses the stanza to introduce the rural setting that the letter writer inhabits and the fact that he writes to her about nature and the chores he does outside:

In February, digging the garden, planting his potatoes,

he saw the first lapwings return and came indoors

to write to me....

Here the present participles 'digging' and 'planting' suggest that these are two activities he is constantly engaged in or engaged in every February, and there is the strong implication that he is going to write to her about what he has just been doing and the return of the lapwings after their winter migration. Dooley has enough empathy or knows enough about his lifestyle to imagine 'his knuckles singing/as they reddened in the warmth'.

Line 5 is succinct and emphatic and marks a change to the present tense: 'It's not romance, just the way things are.' Dooley then makes clear that the real subject of the poem is the contrast in their lifestyles and she switches to the second person:

You out there, in the cold, seeing the seasons

turning, me with my headful of headlines,

feeding words onto a blank screen.

The alliteration of 'headful of headlines' draws attention to itself and underlines one difference in their life styles: headlines change every day, but watching the seasons turn is a slower, more relaxed activity. He grows potatoes which are eaten; she feeds 'words onto a blank screen'. At the end of the third stanza Dooley asks: 'Is your life more real because you dig and sow?'

In the fourth stanza Dooley states the 'you wouldn't say so' - that he would not agree that his life is more real than hers. However, in the same sentence she includes two very 'real' things that he does which strongly suggests that she thinks his life is more real. The whole quotation reads:

You wouldn't say so, breaking ice on a waterbutt,

clearing a path through the snow.

Once again we notice the present participles – 'breaking', 'clearing' – which suggest these are regular activities, and they are activities which are more physically real than a 'headful of headlines'. There is a tone of gratitude in the next lines which suggest that Dooley feels unhappy in the city and craves the realities of life in the countryside and the realities of the natural world:

it's you

who sends me of that other world

pouring light and air into an envelope.

The last line in this quotation is a metaphor and a very fresh and beautiful one: we all need light and air to see and to breathe – and her friend's letters from Yorkshire perform a vital function in her life. They remind her of the real world of nature, the seasons and physical work – things that she is sheltered from in the city. Dooley claims earlier 'It's not romance' (referring to the relationship), but she seems to regard life in the countryside as romantic and it provides her with 'light and air' in the sterile environment of the city.

The end of the poem shows their close connection to each other:

at night, watching the same news in different houses,

our souls tap out messages across the icy miles.

'Our souls' – right at the end of the poem Dooley switches to the first person plural to show their closeness and familiarity with one another. It has been suggested that tapping out messages is a reference to Morse code or even to texting, but it is their souls that are sending the messages. Texting is just too banal and mundane – the point surely is that they are so in tune with one another that their souls communicate 'across the icy miles' – the poem ending with a memorable piece of assonance.

Dooley contrasts the two lifestyles very effectively in this poem and in such a way that she makes clear she reveres and misses the real, outdoor life in Yorkshire. Her friends letters are filled with details of what he is doing on the land and the arrival of wildlife – his letters are her source of 'air and light' – which suggests that she finds her current lifestyle suffocating and stultifying. Her job as a journalist deals with news that changes every day; his work in Yorkshire involves repeated actions – he probably plants potatoes every February – but his activities are more in tune with nature and the rhythms of the seasons.

For the most part Dooley uses every-day, straightforward language and little figurative language. She uses quite long sentences and lots of enjambment, so that when she does write a short sentence it stands out and is foregrounded – as she does in lines 5 and 9.

Interestingly the poem raises the question of news. The poet with her 'head full of headlines' works as a newspaper journalist. This is contrasted with the 'news' of the lapwings' arrival after their winter absence and the news that her friend had to break the ice on the water butt. The poem questions what we classify as 'news' – the daily-changing diet of headlines we are fed or the age-old rituals of gardening and farming. Of course, we need and value both, but only one provides us with 'air and light'.

The issue of communication is an important one in the poem. We have already noted that the hand-written personal letters that the poet's friend sends her are old-fashioned in today's world of texts and emails and WhatApp, but it takes more time to write a personal letter, to address it and to take it to the post box to post it – more evidence that the lifestyle of the man is slower and allows him more time and that he takes the time and trouble to write the letters. The poet is a journalist but communicates with headlines – which in the era of online news and news feeds are subject to almost continual change. Finally, in the final line, we reach the poem's climax in which their souls are said to communicate with each other despite their geographical separateness.

'Letters from Yorkshire' by Maura Dooley:

- deals with a platonic, non-romantic relationship between the poet and a man who lives in Yorkshire;

- contrasts her sterile urban existence and her job with the natural rhythms of life and his work in the countryside (which Dooley presents as more real and satisfying);

- poses the question of what we classify and value as 'news';

- explores different ways of communicating.

'Eden Rock' – Charles Causley

Context

Charles Stanley Causley, CBE, FRSL (24 August 1917 – 4 November 2003) was a Cornish poet, schoolmaster and writer. His work is noted for its simplicity and directness and for its associations with folklore, especially when linked to his native Cornwall. At a time when poetry was becoming experimental and often very esoteric, Causley persisted with traditional forms (as he does in this poem), and breathed fresh life into them.

somewhere beyond – a suitably vague location.

a sprigged dress – embroidered with representations of twigs.

a screw of paper – a scrunched wad of paper which acts as a cork.

from the other bank – his parents are the other side of the stream, but, as we shall see, this phrase has deeper connotations.

Who? Charles Causley and his parents.

When? The poem is written in the present tense, but Causley appears to be looking back with affectionate nostalgia on past events.

Where? Eden Rock – a picturesque location that Causley invented for the sake of the poem. The choice of 'Eden' suggests paradise and this links with the intense nostalgia in most of the poem.

What? In the poem his parents are having a picnic and inviting him to cross a stream to join them.

Commentary

Most readers treat this poem as a simple exercise in nostalgia and an expression of love and affection for his parents. Certainly on one level, the poem works like this, but (as we shall see) there are other elements in the poem which work to make it more than a simple nostalgia narrative.

In the first stanza Causley's parents are waiting for him 'Somewhere beyond Eden Rock' – a suitably mysterious location. The first two stanzas establish that his parents are relatively young too and even his father's dog is 'still two years old'. His mother lays a table cloth over the grass and pours tea from a Thermos. There is the affectionate memory of trivial details which give a sense of verisimilitude: the milk 'in an old H.P. Sauce bottle' and 'the same three plates, the tin cups painted blue'. His father wears the 'same suit', but the same suit as what? The same suit that Causley remembers seeing him in often?

This is presented as a familiar scene from Causley's childhood, and he uses the present tense to give it immediacy and vibrancy, but it seems as if he is writing about a time before he was born. He is physically separated from his parents and before his mother looks at him, 'The sky whitens as if lit by three suns' – a strange and momentous image.

In the final stanza his parents call to him:

They beckon to me from the other bank,

I hear them call, 'See where the stream path is!

Crossing is not as hard as you might think.'

Before we consider the final line, we should consider the form of the poem. Causley writes in regular quatrains, but uses different types of half-rhyme at the end of every line – in fact, he only uses full rhyme at the end with 'this' and 'is'. Half-rhyme is often used by poets when they want to suggest something is wrong.

And certainly something is wrong. After all the nostalgic images, Causley's clear affection for his parents and the idyllic surroundings, the last line introduces a sinister note of unease which is foregrounded by the line being not physically part of the final stanza – the line's isolation suggesting the poet's isolation or sense of isolation:

I did not think it would be like this.

This line is vague, but it is totally at odds with the cheery optimism of the rest of the poem and suggests that 'it', life, has been very different from what Causley expected – it has not been one long picnic in the moors 'somewhere beyond Eden Rock'. His parents did not stay twenty-five and twenty-three forever. Indeed, it is quite possible that Causley wrote this poem after their deaths – the underworld is separated from the land of the living by a stream as Causley is in the poem. Thinking about the title it is worth remembering that, although the Garden of Eden was Paradise, Adam and Eve were ejected from Eden. The image of the sky whitening as if 'lit by three suns' inevitably suggests the atomic bombs that were dropped on Hiroshima and Nagasaki.

In the poem Causley's parents are frozen in a time before he was born, having a picnic and waiting for him to join them in life – a life in which they will go on similar picnics – but not for long. Causley was born in 1917 and his father, who fought in the First World War, died of his wounds when Causley was only seven – a devastating loss for one so young. If Causley's father died when he was seven, there cannot have been many family picnics like the one described in the poem. Perhaps the scene that Causley describes is imaginary – one he wishes he had had, but did not because of his father's early death. During the Second World War Causley served in the Royal Navy – an experience that affected him profoundly and as a writer in the 1950s and 1960s he was well aware of the threat of nuclear weapons.

Therefore, what appears as a nostalgic tribute to his parents, is really an elegy to them and to all the horrors of life in the twentieth century. As Causley puts it in stunningly simple English:

I did not think it would be like this.

As readers we realize that the idyllic picnic beyond Eden Rock probably never happened except in Causley's imagination – which adds to the sense of devastation and loss at the end of the poem.

An alternative reading might be that Causley's parents are dead, frozen in the ages at which he remembers them, and that they are calling to him from beyond the grave in a picnic scene that Causley remembers. We are still left with the unsettling and devastating last line – 'I did not think it would be like this', in which the simple monosyllabic words, completely devoid of any figurative language – spell out a harsh and threatening truth. What does Causley mean by 'it'? The answer is surely simple – life, human existence, the world as it is.

In 'Eden Rock' Charles Causley

- uses a simple form to write what appears to be a poem of nostalgia about childhood;

- writes not a tribute to his parents or to his childhood, but an elegy to them and the lost innocence of his childhood world;

- in his devastating last line combines the deeply personal with the wider implications of being alive in the 20th century;

- uses the simile 'as if lit by three suns' to move the poem to a higher level and to ensure the poem moves beyond family picnics – which probably never happened as described in the poem.

'Follower' – Seamus Heaney

Context

Seamus Heaney was born on 13 April 1939 and died on 30 August 2013. Heaney was an Irish poet, widely recognized as one of the best poets writing in English in the late 20th and early 21st centuries. He was awarded the Nobel Prize for Literature in 1995. He was born and brought up in Northern Ireland, but lived in the Republic of Ireland from 1973. Heaney considered himself an Irish poet and objected to being included in collections of 'British' poets. Northern Ireland has had a violent and troubled history, but Heaney's poems (even those which do address political concerns) are always deeply personal and rooted in everyday events and circumstances. This poem (first published in 1966 in the collection *Death of a Naturalist*) explores his relationship with his father – as do several other poems in that collection.

the shafts – the two parallel wooden handles that the ploughman uses to control the direction of the plough.

the furrow – the trench made by a plough.

the wing – the stabilizers on either side of the plough.

sock – the ploughshare – the sharpened metal that cuts through the soil.

headrig – a headland in a ploughed field.

the sweating team – the team of two horses pulling the plough.

the polished sod – the earth upturned by the plough; it is polished because it is damp.

Who? The speaker in the poem is Heaney himself, writing about his father.

When? Most of the poem is set in Heaney's childhood, in the past, but the final sentence brings us sharply back to the present.

Where? In a generalized rural setting.

What? Heaney describes his father's skill and prowess as a ploughman, and the way he idolized him, but in a poignant ending notes that their positions are now reversed. The title, we realize by the end of the poem, is deliberately ambiguous.

Commentary

'Follower' is a well-known poem by Seamus Heaney and it has often been studied at GCSE. There is a reason for that: it is a very good poem and, at its end, very poignant and moving. Heaney was born into a farming family and a large part of the poem is a eulogy or tribute to his father's skill as a ploughman – the way he controlled the horses which pulled the plough, the way he controlled the plough as it cut a furrow in an unploughed field, and his general expertise as a ploughman. The poem ends rather unexpectedly with a reflection on old age and the relationship between father and son.

The poem is divided into 6 four-line stanzas and has a strict rhyme scheme, although Heaney occasionally uses half-rhyme instead of full rhyme. This regularity mimics the precision of the ploughing process which we know has to be precise and at which Heaney's father is 'an expert'. Keeping to a pattern also recalls the fields full of straight furrows after they have been ploughed. The regular rhythm also mimics the movement of the horses pulling the plough and Heaney's father's footsteps plodding behind them.

The poem starts with a simple statement: 'My father worked with a horse-plough' – as in the photo above. 'His shoulders globed like a full sail' contains a simile ('like a full sail') which suggests something large and expansive, but 'globed' is a metaphor which suggests the size and strength of Heaney's father's back, but also suggests his father's importance to him: he is his whole world (globe). His father controls the horses with his 'clicking tongue'. Heaney's understanding of the technical terms to do with ploughing and the parts of the plough – 'shafts', 'furrow', 'wing', 'sock', 'headrig' – suggests the younger Heaney's interest in ploughing.

The second stanza opens with a two word sentence which is foregrounded by being only two words long, but also at the start of the stanza – isolated and drawing attention to itself. The stanza focuses on what Heaney's father does – setting the wing and fitting the sock. Everything is presented in a positive way, even the sod 'rolled over without breaking' and when they reach the end of the field Heaney's father uses 'a single pluck' to make the horses turn around to plough the next furrow.

Not only does Heaney's father possess complete and expert control of the plough and the horses, he also possesses a good eye which

Narrowed and angled at the ground,

Napping the furrow exactly.

Stanza four concentrates on Heaney as a boy. He sometimes stumbled in his father's 'hob-nailed wake' or fell on the 'polished sod': so, in contrast to his father who is an expert, Heaney is a clumsy child.

The fifth stanza conveys a sense of regret. As a young boy, all Heaney wanted to do was to be an expert ploughman like his father: 'to close one eye, stiffen my arm'. He revered and idolized his father so much:

All I ever did was follow

His broad shadow round the farm.

The sixth and final stanza sees Heaney looking back at his childhood and he admits

I was a nuisance, tripping, falling,

Yapping always.

The final sentence is crucial to the impact of the poem and deserves a lot of attention. Note how it switches to the present tense:

But today

It is my father who keeps stumbling

Behind me, and will not go away.

Now their roles are reversed and the title of the poem – 'Follower' could easily refer to both father and son. As parents age they become more dependent on their adult children, and now it is Heaney's father who is a nuisance and will not go away. The followed has become the follower. I think Heaney still respects the good, honest toil and the skill in ploughing, but he has chosen a different path in life – university and the life of a writer. In that sense he has not followed his father in the life of a farmer, as he thought he would as a young boy.

And so what began as a eulogy to Heaney's father and to Heaney's own childhood ambitions becomes a lament on the dependency of old age and the inevitable reversal of roles that occurs between father and son as the father ages. As a result the tone of the poem changes radically. What appeared to be a nostalgic poem about childhood, full of adoration and reverence for his father is transformed by the last sentence into a lament about the inevitable reversal of roles that old age can bring.

'Follower' by Seamus Heaney:

- evokes a strong sense of the skill and physical force required to be a good ploughman;

- successfully presents the reverence and admiration that most young boys feel towards their father;

- shows how childhood ambitions can change;

- demonstrates a detailed knowledge of the technicalities of ploughing;

- in the poignant final sentence shows how the father and son relationship can be reversed.

'Mother, any distance' Simon Armitage

Context

Simon Armitage was born in 1963 in the village of Marsden in West Yorkshire and has spent most of his life in that area. He is a very successful and highly-regarded poet, celebrated for his down-to-earth language and subject matter. His poetry often (but not always) deals with the ordinary incidents and events of modern life and appear to be based on personal experience. However, as his career as a poet has progressed, his subject matter has widened impressively.

pelmets – a fringe or other device for hiding a curtain rod.

Who? Armitage addresses the poem to his mother.

When? The setting is contemporary. The poem was first published in 1993.

Where? In Armitage's new house.

What? Armitage's mother is at the house to help in the process of measuring for curtains etc..

Commentary

This is a poem that explores the poet's relationship with his mother in a witty way through the use of an extended metaphor based on the exploration of space. Despite the witty conceit, Armitage raises important questions – to which many readers will be able to relate - towards the end of the poem.

The setting is mundane and domestic. Armitage and his mother are in his new house taking measurements for curtains, carpets and the like – a task which by its very nature requires two people since 'any distance greater than a single span/requires a second pair of hands'. The poet is faced with 'the acres of the walls, the prairies of the floors' – the huge distances implied by the metaphorical 'acres' and 'prairies' perhaps suggesting Armitage's nervousness at moving out of his parents' home into a home of his own: it is an important step in one's growing independence.

In the second stanza his mother is at the zero end while Armitage unreels the spool of the tape measure, calling back to his mother precise measurements in 'metres, centimetres,' 'back to base' – the first phrase which suggests the world of space exploration. The fact that his mother is the 'base' shows how important she still is in the poet's life. The poet writes that the tape measure feeding out is 'unreeling years between us' – the years that separate them but also all the shared experiences of those years. The second quatrain ends in two single word metaphorical sentences. Anchors keep boats moored in one place, and his mother is his anchor because she provides him with stability in stormy weather, difficult times. By contrast, Armitage is a kite, borne aloft by the wind and flying free, but still attached by a line to his mother. The tape measure also represents all the years that Armitage and his mother have shared which also strengthens the familial bond between them.

The sestet begins with Armitage space-walking 'through the empty bedrooms', the tape measure is now metaphorically the line that attaches an astronaut to his spaceship and provides him with oxygen. Armitage makes no explicit reference to it, but the reader cannot help feeling that the tape also represents the umbilical cord that joins a mother to her baby – a connection between mother and child that never ceases to exist.

Armitage climbs the ladder into the loft, while down below his mother's 'fingertips still pinch/the last one hundredth of an inch'. The poet feels he is 'at breaking point, where something has to give'. Then the poem ends

> *…I reach*
>
> *towards a hatch that opens on an endless sky*
>
> *to fall or fly.*

The 'endless sky' represents all the possibilities and promises of an adult, independent existence, and, in a show of brave honesty, the poet admits he may fall to earth and metaphorically die or he may fly – live a successful independent existence, while keeping his relationship with his mother intact. 'To fall or fly' is a beautifully succinct way of expressing these alternatives (foregrounded by the alliteration on *f*), and the metaphor of being an astronaut walking in space builds up to the final line.

The poem begins with a regular rhyme scheme in the first quatrain, but this formality breaks down as the poem progresses with irregular line lengths especially in the third verse. In some ways, despite its irregularity, it resembles a sonnet with two quatrains followed by a sestet and an extra, short, fifteenth line. This breaking down of formality on Armitage's part is deliberate: it reflects the growing uncertainty and uneasiness he feels as he gets further and further from his mother and 'base camp'. It is a perfect example of form mirroring content as he moves from a formal, structured opening to an irregular panicky sestet and leaves all rules of formality behind. This mirrors both his continued need for his mother and his nervousness about setting up house on his own. The poem even begins in a verbally formal way with the use of 'Mother' and 'requires'.

Simon Armitage's 'Mother any distance':

- presents the closeness of the mother/child relationship. Armitage may be an adult setting up home on his own, but he still needs his mother;

- uses the tape measure as a shifting symbol – umbilical cord, mountaineering rope and oxygen supply tube when Armitage introduces the idea of an astronaut on a space-walk;

- uses form and its disintegration to suggest the nervousness and disquiet that Armitage feels;

- ends with a potentially frightening image that we all must face when we leave home and start independent lives – 'to fall or fly;

- implies an affectionate tenderness between mother and son, and a reluctance on Armitage's part to let go, while recognizing that he must become an independent adult.

'Before You Were Mine' – Carol Ann Duffy

Context

Carol Ann Duffy is one of the UK's most successful and best-known living poets. Her poems have a very wide appeal. On May 1ˢᵗ 2009 she became the nation's Poet Laureate – the first woman ever to hold the position. Her poems are often set for study by the examination boards – because they are thought of very highly and because many of them are very accessible. Her poems often use very modern and everyday language, but in fresh, funny and witty ways. She uses traditional forms like the sonnet and the dramatic monologue, but succeeds in breathing new life into these old forms by the modernity of her writing and subject matter. The accessibility of many of her poems may obscure the fact that she is highly skilled at a very intricate and ingenious manipulation of language.

Marilyn – a reference to a famous photo of Marilyn Monroe.

the ballroom with a thousand eyes – the mirror ball that hangs down from the centre of the ceiling at dances and discos, although the 'thousand eyes' may be the five hundred pairs of men's eyes looking at the women at the dance and checking them out.

relics – here venerated objects that once belonged to someone revered and famous: Duffy's mother's red shoes.

George Square – a famous and lively square in Glasgow city centre.

Portobello – a famous beach in an eastern suburb of Edinburgh.

Who? Duffy addresses her mother directly in this poem.

When? In the past – Duffy is trying to recreate through words her mother's life before she gave birth to the poet.

Where? Duffy's mother grew up and lived in Glasgow, so most of the poem is set in Glasgow.

What? The poem acts as a homage to her mother's life before she became pregnant along with a recognition of the responsibilities that being a mother brings and the changes to one's lifestyle that being a parent necessitates.

Commentary

'Before You Were Mine' is a joyous and exuberant celebration of the life of Carol Ann Duffy's mother before the poet was born. As such Duffy lovingly tries to recreate the scenes and the atmosphere of those years, before Duffy herself was born.

The poem opens in the present tense ten years before Duffy's birth – 'I'm ten years from the corner you laugh on /with your pals, Maggie McGeeney and Jean Duff'. The use of specific names gives the poem added intimacy and verisimilitude. The three girls are in high spirits on an evening out and 'shriek at the pavement' because they are in such an excited frame of mind. In the last line of the stanza Duffy writes 'Your polka dot dress blows round your legs. Marilyn'. With one word – 'Marilyn' – Duffy evokes the glamourous image of the film star Marilyn Monroe and also refers to an iconic photograph (see above) of her: she is suggesting that her mother was as glamourous in her own way as Marilyn Monroe and shared the same enthusiasm for life.

The second stanza is in the present tense and starts with a simple statement – 'I'm not here yet' – to remind us that Duffy is not alive, although she is writing about her mother's life as if she were. Duffy's mother is so preoccupied with the "ballroom with the thousand eyes, the fizzy, movie tomorrows/the right walk home could bring' that 'the thought of me doesn't occur'. The 'right walk home' is with a good-looking man and it conjures up images of a better and exciting future – the 'fizzy, movie tomorrows' – ending in love and marriage as many movies of the time did. Her mother always gets home late to find her own mother standing 'at the close [the entrance to their flat] with a hiding [a beating] for the late one'. Duffy comments, with a tone of admiration at her mother's rebelliousness and vivacity: 'You figure it's worth it' – worth it for the 'right walk home' with a handsome man.

The third stanza's first line brings the reality of motherhood a little closer:

The decade ahead of my loud, possessive yell was the best one, eh?

The informal 'eh?' at the end of the line establishes mother and daughter's intimacy and the informal closeness that exists between them, as though Duffy's mother has shared many intimate memories of those years with Duffy. In the next sentence Duffy is writing as an adult looking back on her childhood when she used to play with her mother's eye-catching red shoes: 'I remember my hands in those high-heeled red shoes' which are now treated as 'relics' of her mother's youthful days. She then claims to see her mother's ghost, the ghost of her youthful self, 'clear as scent' (the scent she is wearing) coming clattering (on her high heels) towards the poet in George Square. Her mother in the past seems to be fresh from some romantic encounter and the stanza ends with Duffy asking her 'whose small love bites [are] are on your neck, sweetheart?' The use of 'sweetheart' is interesting: on one hand, it is a term of genuine endearment from Duffy to her mother, but on the other it is the word that the men who chase her might well use to address her.

Stanza four starts with an onomatopoeic attempt to render dance steps which Duffy's mother taught her 'on the way home from Mass'. Her mother is said to be 'stamping stars from the wrong pavement' and this metaphor sums up her mother: the stars are glamourous; 'stamping' suggests an inner strength; and 'the wrong pavement' suggests her non-conformity. Even then 'before I was born' Duffy writes, I wanted 'the

200

bold girl winking in Portobello' – bold and winking at men she fancies, we assume. The last sentence of the poem is a brilliant ending to what precedes it:

That glamourous love lasts

Where you sparkle and waltz and laugh before you were mine.

The last words of the poem neatly use the title itself, and Duffy asserts her love for her mother and her love and reverence for her mother's younger self.

The poem is written in a familiar, confidential and informal way with many contractions, single word sentences and interjections from normal speech – 'eh?' The conceit of pretending to know about her life before Duffy was born is witty in itself and the present tense allows the reader to accept this idea. Some readers have suggested that the poem is inspired by old photos of Duffy and her friends; I think the detail comes from anecdotes – things that Duffy's mother has told her with, perhaps, some invented details.

Despite the youthful joy and exuberance that are celebrated in the poem, there is something else going on: Duffy's love for her mother is very possessive as the possessive pronoun – mine – in the title suggests. She also refers to her 'loud, possessive yell' – being a parent brings with it enormous responsibilities. The poem seems to suggest that Duffy is slightly jealous that she did not know her mother when she was younger – she certainly falls in love with the image of her mother from the time before she was born. Duffy uses imagery of colour, smell and light to romanticize her mother's earlier life before she gave birth to her daughter.

In 'Before You Were Mine' Carol Ann Duffy:

- writes a eulogy to her mother's younger self;

- associates her mother with glamourous images of light and of famous actresses;

- writes a joyous poem of youthful sexual exuberance;

- also shows the possessive love that a child can have for its parent and the difficulties of being a mother.

'Winter Swans' – Owen Sheers

Context

Owen Sheers is a Welsh poet, author and scriptwriter. He has published two poetry collections, *The Blue Book* and *Skirrid Hill* which won a Somerset Maugham Award. His debut prose work *The Dust Diaries*, a non-fiction narrative set in Zimbabwe won the Welsh Book of the Year 2005. Owen's first novel, Resistance has been translated into ten languages. Owen co-wrote the screenplay for the film adaptation, released in the UK in 2011. In 2009 he published the novella White Ravens, a contemporary response to the myth of Branwen Daughter of Llyr, as part of Seren's 'New Stories from the Mabinogion series.

Owen's theatrical writing includes his libretto for Rachel Portman's oratorio, *The Water Diviner's Tale*, which premiered at the Royal Albert Hall for the BBC Proms in 2007. *Unicorns*, almost a one man play about the life and work of WWII poet Keith Douglas, was developed with Old Vic, New Voices. In Easter 2011 Owen wrote the script and novelization (*The Gospel of Us*) for *The Passion*, National Theatre of Wales' 72 hour site-specific production in Port Talbot starring and directed by Michael Sheen. The Observer described the production as 'the theatrical event of the decade'. Owen's short play *The Fair & Tender* was performed as part of the Bush Theatre's 66 Books.

tipping – when swans feed they immerse the top half of their bodies – head, bill, neck and all - at 90 degrees to the lower half of their bodies, so that only the bottom half of their body is visible, sticking up out of the water. This known as tipping.

in unison - simultaneously

stilling – in the act of becoming still; an original and striking usage.

Who? The speaker of the poem and his or her lover.

When? The poem was published in 2005 in the collection *Skirrid Hill*.

Where? Unspecified – but near a lake where swans swim.

What? The speaker of the poem reflects on his/her relationship with his or her lover.

Commentary

The first stanza makes it clear that it has been raining incessantly for two days. In a break in the rain the lovers take a walk. Note Sheers' use of alliteration in the final line which highlights the couple's lack of communication. Given what follows in the rest of the poem, it is tempting to see the 'two days of rain' as a pathetic fallacy for the state of their relationship. The 'waterlogged earth' is 'gasping for breath' as if fighting for its very existence in Sheers' personification of it; perhaps their relationship is also 'gasping for breath'. The lovers 'skirted the lake', 'silent and apart'; 'skirted' can mean to go round the edge of something – in this case the lake – but you can also skirt round an issue – perhaps an issue the couple don't want to confront. Certainly the couple are 'silent and apart' – perhaps they have nothing to say to each other or perhaps they know that they will bicker if they try to communicate.

In the third stanza the swans 'came and stopped us' with 'a show of tipping in unison'. Swans are remarkably beautiful and elegant birds, even when engaged in the simple act of feeding. In the UK swans enjoy the protection of the Crown – all unmarked swans belong to the Queen – and as a result they are not hunted. Swans are a part of Western culture, often occurring in fairy tale or myth. The movement of swans tipping is so elegant the speaker wonders (in a simile) whether they are 'rolling weights down their bodies to their heads'. To the onlooker it appears that they have 'halved themselves in the dark water'; in a metaphor they are compared to 'icebergs of white feather' before they re-emerge from the water 'like boats righting in rough weather'. If swans and boats can right themselves (return to an upright position), then perhaps there is a chance that the couple can return to a state of happiness and equilibrium.

As the swans fly off, Sheers allows the speaker's lover to speak: "They mate for life,' you said. Having been compared to icebergs (big and dangerous and white), Sheers uses a much more fragile and beautiful metaphor to describe the swans – they are 'porcelain over the stilling lake'. Porcelain is a fragile but beautiful creation. 'Stilling' is an original and interesting usage: 'stilling' gives the impression that the water is slowly and gradually becoming still.

The speaker does not reply to the point about swans mating for life and they continue to walk around the lake, but whereas before they had skirted the lake they now are now 'slow-stepping' – together and slowly – just as the swans tipped in unison, The last sentence of the poem is long and a real tour-de-force, leading up to the climax in the last line.

The speaker notices that as they have walked slowly along the 'lake's shingle and sand',

…our hands that had somehow,

swum the distance between us,

and folded, one over the other,

like a pair of wings settling after flight

This ending is rich in metaphors and Sheers ensures they are closely related to swans and water. Their hands swim between them to hold each other's hand; the hands fold over one another as a swan's wings fold over one another and the final simile 'like a pair of wings settling after flight' suggests strongly a reconciliation between the two lovers prompted by the sight of the swans and the remark that they mate for life. The lovers' hands settling after flight become one joined set of wings, united and reconciled. After the flight of their disagreements, they have now settled into reconciliation. However, observant readers will notice that Sheers omits the full stop at the end of the final sentence: is this to suggest that not all the couple's problems have been resolved and that they face further 'rainy days' ahead?

This is a poem about reconciliation and the catalysts for the reconciliation are the swans. The swans are beautiful in themselves; their tipping is a graceful motion and the simile Sheers uses to get them upright again – 'like boats righting in rough weather' – demonstrates to the couple that things can be righted. Then comes the observation that swans are monogamous (as are several species of birds). The lovers hands reunite in a metaphor drawn from water – 'they had swum the distance between us' – and the hands folded over remind us of the swans – 'like a pair of wings settling after flight'; the 'flight' in this case being the couple's lack of communication at the start of the poem. The lovers have learnt from the swans, and the sight and grace of the swans have encouraged their reconciliation, although that reconciliation is subdued and delicately tentative –as the missing full stop implies.

The location deserves attention. The poet uses a lake in winter and uses the weather to suggest what has been going on in the relationship. 'The clouds had given their all' – it has rained incessantly for two days and the ground is waterlogged. After the swans depart, the water on the lake is 'stilling' – calm is being restored to the landscape and to the relationship: their walk slows and their hands come together.

The poem is written in free verse with occasional internal rhyme. The first six stanzas all have three lines, but the last poem has two – mirroring the two hands that are now joined together as closely as a swan's wings.

Owen Sheers' 'Winter Swans' is:

- a tender poem which enacts a tentative reconciliation between two lovers;

- uses the swans as both a metaphor and a catalyst for the reconciliation achieved at the end of the poem;

- matches the visual elegance of the swans with a restrained elegance of the words, especially in the beautiful last stanza.

'Singh Song!' – Daljit Nagra

Context

Daljit Nagra was born in 1966 to Punjabi Indian parents. He has been hailed as one of the most exciting poets of his generation. His first collection *Look We Have Coming to Dover!* is full of monologues which attempt to capture the experience in Britain of the Indian working classes. His poetry is preoccupied with what it is like to be an Asian growing up and living in Britain, so his work touches on issues of belonging, identity, racism, but also what it means to be British. It is a stereotype of Indian-ness that they run corner shops; when many Indians first arrived in the UK, it was certainly one quick and legitimate way for them to establish themselves in business, because they could buy a corner shop and run it as they chose without any barriers because of their race.

he vunt me – he wants me.

chapatti – unleavened Indian bread.

chutney – another staple of Indian cuisine. A side dish made from fruit or vegetables and designed to be eaten with bread or poppadoms.

Putney – apart from being an area of South West London, 'putney' is also the Punjabi word for 'wife'. Putney is on the Thames and lots of rowing clubs practise there. Every year the river at Putney hosts the Oxford and Cambridge Boat Race.

effing – swearing profusely.

di tickle of my bride – a euphemism for sex.

di brighty moon – clearly this means the moon is bright, but there may be a play on words. 'Brighty' is very similar to the word 'Blighty' which British people used to use as a word signifying Great Britain. 'Blighty' itself is the Hindi word for 'home'.

Who? The narrator is Singh, an Indian shopkeeper who runs one of his father's shops. There are references to his parents, to his new bride and to the customers of his shop. The poem is a dramatic monologue because the poet adopts a voice which is clearly not his own.

When? Now – in the early 21st century. The poem describes a typical day for the narrator and ends in the evening when the moon is visible.

Where? In the narrator's father's shop and the flat upstairs where his new bride waits for him. The mention of Putney in line 9 suggests it might be set in south west London, but the word 'putney' has other connotations. It is the Punjabi word for wife and, bearing in mind the strenuous activity involved in rowing, the simile 'like we rowing through Putney' is very sexual in its connotations and suggests very strenuous sex.

What? Singh describes his day in the shop and the time he spends with his wife upstairs in the flat. Apart from two italicized interjections by the dissatisfied voices of his customers, this is a dramatic monologue as Nagra adopts a voice that is not his.

Commentary

In this amusing yet ultimately tender poem, Nagra adopts the voice of a young Indian man in the UK who runs one of his father's corner shops. This partly corresponds to a racial stereotype about Indians running corner shops in urban or suburban areas. Nagra embraces the stereotype and reveals a truth behind the image. Although the overall effect is deeply funny, the poem also raises serious questions about identity and culture.

The title of the poem is a pun. The narrator is a Sikh and Singh is a common Sikh name; in addition, many people say that Indians speak English in a sing-song manner because of the rhythm in which they speak English. So it is the song of Singh and it also reflects the way he speaks: throughout the poem Nagra uses phonetic spelling to imitate Singh's accent and his use of half-rhyme and full rhyme increase the poem's song-like qualities as do the two italicized verses where Singh's customers speak, providing a sort of chorus to the main part of the poem which is Singh's description of his life.

The opening two stanzas tell us about the narrator's situation: he runs one of his father's shops and is expected to be open from nine in the morning until nine at night. But when there are no customers Singh shuts the shop and goes upstairs to make love to his wife. He prioritizes love over business. In the poem he and his wife reject the traditional values of business which his father and mother's generation hold so dear. Singh tells us that 'from 9 o'clock to 9 o'clock/and he [his father] vunt me not to have a break', but he takes frequent breaks to go upstairs to make love to his wife. The stereotype that Nagra is subverting is that of the well-run Indian corner shop, managed by someone in the family, and open and accessible at all hours.

The third stanza describes what happens when he returns downstairs to the shop. The lines in italics are the voices of his customers who pour out a litany of complaints about his shop, concluding that Singh's is

... *di worst Indian shop*

on di whole Indian road.

The next three stanzas are devoted to his new wife and we can see that he is totally obsessed with her. Each stanza begins *my bride* – which suggests they have not been married for very long. He hears her high heels tapping above his head and imagines her flirting with other men on a Sikh dating website. He seems to get vicarious pleasure from this – knowing that other men find her attractive. There is a funny play on words: Singh's wife

...is playing wid mouse

ven she netting two cat on her Sikh lover site

she book them for the meat at the cheese ov her price

The cat and mouse (the computer mouse) imagery and the cheese suggest she catches men who are motivated by sexual attraction (meat). Far from being jealous, Singh seems proud of his new bride's ability to do this. There has even been a suggestion that she is running a dating agency for Sikhs. Cheese and meat are also used because they may well be products sold in Singh's shop.

Singh's wife seems to show no respect to his parents:

she effing at my mum

in all di colours of Punjabi

den stumble like a drunk

malking fun at my daddy.

In the next stanza she is described in contrasting similes that suggest both danger on the one hand and cuteness on the other: his wife has

tiny eyes of a gun

and the tummy of a teddy

His wife deliberately rebels against the expectations of Singh's parents. She has a 'red crew cut' and the clothes she wears (a Tartan sari) suggest she has absorbed some parts of Western culture, while rejecting the work ethic of her husband's parents' generation. Her hair style and her tartan sari can be seen as signs of assimilation, but are also visually funny; as is the donkey jacket she wears. She mimics his father too – showing a lack of respect. We can imagine that Singh's father runs a very efficient shop which is clean and where the bread is not stale and the milk is not out of date.

The customers' voices are heard again complaining about the products in the shop – Singh has neglected all this because he would rather be upstairs making love to his wife. The customers complain that Singh's shop is

...di worst Indian shop

In de whole Indian road

I do not think this is intended to be racist. It is race-related, because of the stereotype of Indians running corner shops, but in the poem Singh would be the first to admit that he does not care about the shop – he shuts it in order to make love to his new bride, when the whole idea of such a shop is that it is open all hours. In fact, Singh's laziness over the shop and his enthusiasm for his new bride both undercut the stereotype of the Indian corner shop owner who is only and exclusively concerned with business.

Line 43 begins a lovely romantic interlude. At midnight, Singh says, he and his wife 'cum down whispering stairs' to sit together on the stool behind the counter and stare out of the shop's windows. The shop is part of a precinct which is 'concrete cold' at night and suggests an uninspiring urban location. Beyond the shop window, beyond the community which criticizes Singh's abilities as a shopkeeper and they see

all di beaches ov di UK in de brightey moon.

They stare past

... di half-price window signs

which suggests they do not care about them.

We then hear his wife speak for the first time in the poem. She asks him

How much do yoo charge for dat moon baby?

He tells her it is half the price of her and that in itself is priceless, so she must be doubly priceless. And so the poem ends on a note of intense romantic tenderness.

His wife's question is deliberately couched in financial terms: corner shops might have all sorts of offers – things that are half-price or on special offer or three for the price of two, but true love and passion cannot be bought and sold and has no price.

Singh does not care about running his shop efficiently; he only cares about his wife and her pleasure. This is a love poem and a poem about rebelling against the expectations of your parents and the community.

Why?

This hilarious poem is full of tender, romantic love

- explores the cultural fusion of second generation British Indians;

- rejects the work ethic and materialism of older generations;

- shows a character rejecting the role picked out for him by his father;

- imitates accent and uses non-Standard English to give us an authentic sense of character and culture;

- subverts traditional stereotypes of British-Asian behaviour;

- is comic and exuberant, while also giving a sense that the couple feel trapped by the shop they run;

- presents a couple engaged in a fulfilling and loving relationship.

'Climbing My Grandfather' – Andrew Waterhouse

Context

Andrew Waterhouse (27 November 1958 Lincolnshire - 20 October 2001) was a British poet, and musician. He grew up in Scarborough and moved to Gainsborough where his parents ran the local Conservative Club, the river allotments and paved streets which feature in his early poetry are all still where he would have remembered them, and he was educated at Gainsborough Grammar School. He studied at Newcastle University, and Wye College, taking an MSc. in environmental science. He lectured at Kirkley Hall Agricultural College. Drawing on his background in this semi-industrial town his early poetry reflects on the town and his family and is evocative of the period (1970s) and the place. He wrote for green journals, and took part in the Trees for Life programme for world reforestation. In 2001 he took his own life.

brogues – a stout, solid shoe.

traverse – a passage across the face of a rock in mountaineering.

good purchase – a good, solid grip.

screed – a smooth area.

Who? Waterhouse imagines himself as very, very tiny and, in a witty extended metaphor, imagines his grandfather as a mountain which he climbs.

When? No specific time.

Where? No specific place.

What? Climbing carefully – with several words from mountaineering – Waterhouse finally reaches the summit – his grandfather's head!

Commentary

Andrew Waterhouse's 'Climbing My Grandfather' is a delightful poem, full of love and nostalgia based around a single extended metaphor or conceit: that the grandfather is a mountain and that the poet or speaker is a mountaineer. The main focus is the grandfather, but the poem makes use of several words from the world of mountaineering or climbing to keep the metaphor going. The extended metaphor is a witty conceit and Waterhouse (although he uses the present tense to give a sense of immediacy) must be writing about a time when he was very small and his grandfather was relatively huge in his young eyes. Of course, for the extended metaphor to make complete sense we must imagine that Waterhouse is very, very tiny in comparison with the mountain that is his grandfather.

The poem opens with a statement of intent in the present tense which at once brings a sense of immediacy to the poem:

I decide to do it free, without a rope or net.

Free climbing is a form of rock climbing specifically contrasted with aid climbing. Like aid climbing, it may use ropes and other means of climbing protection, but only to protect against injury during falls, and not to assist progress. Ropes can be used in free climbing but not to aid upward progress – which must be achieved solely by the mountaineer's hands.

He first makes his way onto his grandfather's sturdy shoes – his brogues and from there 'scramble[s] onto his trousers'. He is scrambling, of course, because he is free climbing. He pushes into his trousers, 'trying to get a grip', a handhold. His grandfather is presented with some vocabulary that would also suit a mountain – 'his <u>overhanging</u> shirt' – like an overhanging crag.

Then in another word specific to mountaineering he 'traverse[s] along his belt/to an earth-stained hand; suggesting that his grandfather is a keen gardener. He tells us that the nails are splintered and give 'good purchase' – and 'good purchase' is essential if you are free climbing. In an oxymoronic simile we are told his grandfather's skin on his fingers is like 'warm ice': his living fingers are alive and warm, but ice continues the mountaineering metaphor, since the higher you climb the more likely you are to encounter ice and snow.

Waterhouse discovers the 'glassy ridge of a scar' on his grandfather's arm, but 'place my feet gently in the old stitches and move on.' He rests for a while 'at his firm shoulder', but I very careful not to look down because 'climbing has its dangers'. He then pulls himself up by the loose skin of his grandfather's neck and stops at his mouth – 'to drink among teeth' – a metaphor which suggests he gives his grandfather a kiss.

'Refreshed' he continues upwards across the 'screed cheek'. He stares into his grandfather's brown eyes, before going up over the forehead and finding the wrinkles there offer numerous handholds and are 'well-spaced and easy.' He reaches his grandfather's 'thick hair (soft and white at this altitude)' and finally reaches the summit. The white hair clearly represents the snow that is found at the top of high mountains. Exhausted and elated by his climb, 'gasping for breath', he lies down in contentment:

Watching clouds and birds circle,

Feeling his heat, knowing

The slow pulse of his good heart.

'Climbing My Grandfather' is written as one extended stanza with regular line lengths but does not use rhyme. It is given coherence by the extended metaphor and Waterhouse's consistent use of words from mountains and from climbing.

The speaker's act is brave: he chooses to climb free and keeps on going at high altitudes, even when he encounters metaphorical ice and snow. We don't learn much about the grandfather but his tolerance is implied:

in the extended metaphor he allows his grandson to climb him. And, equally, the grandson shows respect for his grandfather – he places his feet 'gently in the old stitches of the scar on his arm. He also shows affection by kissing him.

'Climbing My Grandfather' is based on a witty extended metaphor which is inherently amusing, but it is much more than that. In one sense it can be seen as a tribute to mountaineering – especially free climbing – and the vocabulary that Waterhouse uses demonstrates that. Much more importantly, it is a tribute to the poet's grandfather and the love the poet has for him and for his 'good heart'.

Andrew Waterhouse's 'Climbing My Grandfather':

- uses a witty extended metaphor to explore his relationship with his grandfather;

- is a tribute to the love he felt for his grandfather and his grandfather's 'good heart';

- also displays a passion for climbing and mountaineering;

- exudes a tone of genial good humour;

- presents love in a family across the generations;

- overall has a tone of light-hearted playfulness which comes from the slightly surreal nature of the poem's extended metaphor.

Glossary

The Oxford Concise Dictionary of Literary Terms has been invaluable in writing this section of the book. I would again remind the reader that knowledge of these terms is only the start – do NOT define a word you find here in the examination. You can take it for granted that the examiner knows the term: it is up to you to try to use it confidently and with precision and to explain why the poet uses it or what effect it has on the reader.

ALLITERATION   the repetition of the same sounds – usually initial consonants or stressed syllables – in any sequence of closely adjacent words.

ALLUSION   an indirect or passing reference to some event, person, place or artistic work which is not explained by the writer, but which relies on the reader's familiarity with it.

AMBIGUITY   openness to different interpretations.

ANAPHORA

ASSONANCE   the repetition of similar vowel sounds in neighbouring words.

BALLAD   a folk song or orally transmitted poem telling in a simple and direct way a story with a tragic ending. Ballads are normally composed in quatrains with the second and fourth lines rhyming. Such quatrains are known as the ballad stanza because of its frequent use in what we call ballads.

BLANK VERSE   unrhymed lines of ten syllable length. This is a widely used form by Shakespeare in his plays, by Milton and by Wordsworth.

CAESURA	any pause in a line of verse caused by punctuation. This can draw attention to what precedes or follows the caesura and also, by breaking up the rhythm of the line, can slow the poem down and make it more like ordinary speech.
CANON	a body of writings recognized by authority. The canon of a national literature is a body of writings especially approved by critics or anthologists and deemed suitable for academic study. Towards the end of the 20th century there was a general feeling that the canon of English Literature was dominated by dead white men and since then there has been a deliberate and fruitful attempt made to give more prominence to writing by women and by writers from non-white backgrounds. Even your Anthology is a contribution to the canon, because someone sat down and decided that the poems included in it were worthy of study by students taking GCSE.
CARPE DIEM	a Latin phrase from the Roman poet Horace which means 'seize the day' – 'make the best of the present moment'. It is a very common theme of European lyric poetry, in which the speaker of a poem argues that since time is short and death is inevitable, pleasure should be enjoyed while there is still time.
COLLOCATION	the act of putting two words together. What this means in practice is that certain words have very common collocations – in other words they are usually found in written or spoken English in collocation with other words. For example, the

word *Christmas* is often collocated with words such as *cards, presents, carols, holidays,* but you won't often find it collocated with *sadness*. This can be an important term because poets, who are seeking to use words in original ways, will often put two words together are not often collocated.

COLLOQUIALISM the use of informal expressions or vocabulary appropriate to everyday speech rather than the formality of writing. When used in poetry it can make the poem seem more down-to-earth and real, more honest and intimate.

CONCEIT an unusually far-fetched metaphor presenting a surprising and witty parallel between two apparently dissimilar things or feelings.

CONSONANCE the repetition of identical or similar consonants in neighbouring words whose vowel sounds are different.

CONTEXT the biographical, social, cultural and historical circumstances in which a text is produced and read and understood – you might to think of it as its background. However, it is important sometimes to consider the reader's own context – especially when we look back at poems from the Literary Heritage. To interpret a poem with full regard to its background is to contextualize it.

COUPLET a pair of rhyming verse lines, usually of the same length.

CROSSED RHYME the rhyming of one word in the middle of a long line of poetry with a word in a similar position in the next line.

DIALECT
a distinctive variety of language, spoken by members of an identifiable regional group, nation or social class. Dialects differ from one another in pronunciation, vocabulary and grammar. Traditionally they have been looked down on and viewed as variations from an educated 'standard' form of the language, but linguists point out that standard forms themselves are merely dialects which have come to dominate for social and political reasons. In English this notion of dialect is especially important because English is spoken all over the world and there are variations between the English spoken in, say, Yorkshire, Delhi and Australia. Dialects now are increasingly celebrated as a distinct way of speaking and writing which are integral to our identity.

DICTION
the choice of words used in any literary work.

DISSONANCE
harshness of sound.

DRAMATIC MONOLOGUE
a kind of poem in which a single fictional or historical character (not the poet) speaks to a silent audience and unwittingly reveals the truth about their character.

ELEGY
a lyric poem lamenting the death of a friend or public figure or reflecting seriously on a serious subject. The elegiac has come to refer to the mournful mood of such poems.

ELLIPSIS the omission from a sentence of a word or words which would be required for complete clarity. It is used all the time in everyday speech, but is often used in poetry to promote compression and/or ambiguity. The adjective is elliptical.

END-RHYME rhyme occurring at the end of a line of poetry. The most common form of rhyme.

END-STOPPED a line of poetry brought to a pause by the use of punctuation. The opposite of enjambment.

ENJAMBMENT caused by the lack of punctuation at the end of a line of poetry, this causes the sense (and the voice when the poem is read aloud) to 'run over' into the next line. In general, this can impart to poems the feel of ordinary speech, but there are examples in the Anthology of more precise reasons for the poet to use enjambment.

EPIPHANY a sudden moment of insight or revelation, usually at the end of a poem.

EPIZEUXIS the technique by which a word is repeated for emphasis with no other words intervening

EUPHONY a pleasing smoothness of sound

FALLING RHYTHM the effect produced by several lines in succession which end with a feminine ending

FEMININE ENDING the ending of a line of poetry on an unstressed syllable

FIGURATIVE Not literal. Obviously 'figurative' language covers metaphor and simile and personification

FIGURE OF SPEECH any expression which departs from the

ordinary literal sense or normal order of words. Figurative language (the opposite of literal language) includes metaphor, simile and personification. Some figures of speech – such as alliteration and assonance achieve their effects through the repetition of sounds.

FOREGROUNDING — giving unusual prominence to one part of a text. Poetry differs from everyday speech and prose by its use of regular rhythm, metaphors, alliteration and other devices by which its language draws attention to itself.

FREE VERSE — a kind of poetry that does not conform to any regular pattern of line length or rhyme. The length of its lines are irregular as its use of rhyme – if any.

HALF-RHYME — an imperfect rhyme – also known as para-rhyme, near rhyme and slant rhyme – in which the final consonants but the vowel sounds do not match. Pioneered in the 19th century by the Emily Dickinson and Gerard Manley Hopkins, and made even more popular by Wilfred Owen and T S Eliot in the early 20th century,

HOMONYM — a word that is identical to another word either in sound or in spelling

HOMOPHONE — a word that is pronounced in the same way as another word but which differs in meaning and/or spelling.

HYPERBOLE	exaggeration for the sake of emphasis.
IDIOM	an everyday phrase that cannot be translated literally because its meaning does not correspond to the specific words in the phrase. There are thousands in English like – *you get up my nose*, *when pigs fly*, *she was all ears*.
IMAGERY	a rather vague critical term covering literal and metaphorical language which evoke sense impressions with reference to concrete objects – the things the writer describes.
INTERNAL RHYME	a poetic device in which two or more words in the same line rhyme.
INTERTEXTUALITY	the relationship that a text may have with anoth preceding and usually well-known text.
INVERSION	the reversal of the normally expected order or words. 'Normally expected' means how we might say the words in the order of normal speech; to invert the normal word order usually draws attention or foregrounds the words.
JUXTAPOSITION	two things that are placed alongside each other.
LAMENT	any poem expressing profound grief usually in the face of death.
LATINATE	Latinate diction in English means the use of words derived from Latin rather than those derived from Old English.
LITOTES	understatement – the opposite of hyperbole.
LYRIC	any fairly short poem expressing the personal

mood of the speaker.

METAPHOR the most important figure of speech in which in which one thing is referred to by a word normally associated with another thing, so as to suggest some common quality shared by both things. In metaphor, this similarity is directly stated, unlike in a simile where the resemblance is indirect and introduced by the words like or as. Much of our everyday language is made up of metaphor too – to say someone is as greedy as a pig is a simile; to say he is a pig is a metaphor.

MNEMONIC a form of words or letters that helps people remember things. It is common in everyday sayings and uses some of the features of language that we associate with poetry. For example, the weather saying Red sky at night, shepherd's delight uses rhyme.

MONOLOGUE` an extended speech uttered by one speaker.

NARRATOR the one who tells or is assumed to be the voice of the poem.

OCTAVE or OCTET a group of eight lines forming the first part of a sonnet.

ONOMATOPOEIA the use of words that seem to imitate the sounds they refer to (*bang, whizz, crackle, fizz*) or any combination or words in which the sound echoes or seems to echo the sense. The adjective is onomatopoeic, so you can say that *blast* is an onomatopoeic word.

ORAL TRADITION the passing on from one generation to another of songs, chants, poems, proverbs by word of mouth and memory.

OXYMORON a figure of speech that combines two seemingly contradictory terms as in the everyday terms bitter-sweet and living death.

PARALLELISM the arrangement of similarly constructed clause, sentences or lines of poetry.

PARADOX a statement which is self-contradictory.

PATHETIC FALLACY this is the convention that natural phenomena (usually the weather) are a reflection of the poet's or the narrator's mood. It may well involve the personification of things in nature, but does not have to. At its simplest, a writer might choose to associate very bad weather with a mood of depression and sadness.

PERSONA the assumed identity or fictional narrator assumed by a writer.

PERSONIFICATION a figure of speech in which animals, abstract ideas or lifeless things are referred to as if they were human. Sometimes known as personal metaphor.

PETRARCHAN characteristic of the Italian poet Petrarch (1304 – 1374). Mainly applied to the Petrarchan sonnet which is different in its form from the Shakespearean sonnet.

PHONETIC SPELLING a technique writers use which involves misspelling a word in order to imitate the accent in which the word is said.

PLOSIVE — explosive. Used to describe sounds that we form by putting our lips together such as *b* and *p*.

POSTCOLONIAL LITERATURE — a term devised to describe what used to be called Commonwealth Literature (and before that Empire Writing!). The term covers a very wide range of writing from countries that were once colonies of European countries. It has come to include some writing by writers of non-white racial backgrounds whose roots or family originated in former colonies – no matter where they live now.

PUN — an expression that derives humour either through using a word that has two distinct meanings or two similar sounding words (homophones).

QUATRAIN — a verse stanza of four lines – usually rhymed.

REFRAIN — a line, or a group of lines, repeated at intervals throughout a poem – usually at regular intervals and at the end of a stanza.

RHYME — the identity of sound between syllables or paired groups of syllables usually at the end of a line of poetry.

RHYME SCHEME — the pattern in which the rhymed line endings are arranged in any poem or stanza. This is normally written as a sequence of letters where each line ending in the same rhyme is given the same alphabetical letter. So a Shakespearean sonnet's rhyme scheme is ababcdcdefefgg, but the rhyme scheme of a Petrarchan sonnet is abbaabbacdecde. In other poems the rhyme scheme might be arranged to suit the poet's convenience or intentions. For example, in Blake's 'London' the first stanza rhymes abab, the second cdcd and so on.

RHYTHM   a pattern of sounds which is repeated with the stress falling on the same syllables (more or less) in each line. However, variations to the pattern, especially towards the end of the poem, often stand out and are foregrounded because they break the pattern the poet has built up through the course of the poem.

ROMANTICISM   the name given to the artistic movement that emerged in England and Germany in the 19790a and in the rest of Europe in the 1820s and beyond. It was a movement that saw great changes in literature, painting, sculpture, architecture and music and found its catalyst in the new philosophical ideas of Jean Jacques Rousseau and Thomas Paine, and in response to the French and industrial revolutions. Its chief emphasis was on freedom of individual self-expression, sincerity, spontaneity and originality, but it also looked to the distant past of the Middle Ages for some of its inspiration.

SATIRE   any type of writing which exposes and mocks the foolishness or evil of individuals, institutions or societies. A poem can be satiric (adjective) or you can say a poet satirizes something or somebody.

SESTET — a group of six lines forming the second half of a sonnet, following the octet.

SIBILANCE — the noticeable recurrence of *s* sounds.

SIMILE — an explicit comparison between two different things, actions or feelings, usually introduced by *like* or *as*.

SONNET — a lyric poem of 14 lines of equal length. The form originated in Italy and was made famous as a vehicle for love poetry by Petrarch and came to be adopted throughout Europe. The standard subject matter of early sonnets was romantic love, but in the 17th century John Donne used it to write religious poetry and John Milton wrote political sonnets, so it came to be used for any subject matter. The sonnet form enjoyed a revival in the Romantic period (Wordsworth, Keats and Shelley all wrote them) and continues to be widely used today. Some poets have written connected series of sonnets and these are known as sonnet cycles. Petrarchan sonnets differ slightly in their rhyme scheme from Shakespearean sonnets (see the entry above on rhyme scheme). A Petrarchan sonnet consists of two quatrains (the octet) followed by two tercets (the sestet). A Shakespearean sonnet consist of two quatrains (the octet) followed by another quatrain and a final couplet (the sestet).

STANZA — a group of verse lines forming a section of a poem and sharing the same structure in terms of the length of the lines, the rhyme scheme and the rhythm.

STYLE	any specific way of using language, which is characteristic of an author, a period, a type of poetry or a group of writers.
SYLLOGISM	a form of logical argument that draws a conclusion from two propositions. It is very characteristic of Metaphysical poetry and is exemplified in the anthology by Marvell's 'To His Coy Mistress'.
SYMBOL	anything that represents something else. A national flag symbolizes the country that uses it; symbols are heavily used in road signs. In poetry symbols can represent almost anything. Blake's 'The Sick Rose' and Armitage's 'Harmonium' are two good examples of symbols dealt with in this book.
SYNECDOCHE	a figure of speech in which a thing or person is referred to indirectly, either by naming some part of it (*hands* for manual labourers) or by naming some big thing of which it is a part (the law for police officers). As you can see from these examples, it is a common practice in speech.
TONE	a critical term meaning the mood or atmosphere of a piece of writing. It may also include the sense of the writer's attitude to the reader of the subject matter.
TURN	the English term for a sudden change in mood or line of argument, especially in line 9 of a sonnet.
VERSE	another word for poetry as opposed to prose. The use of the word 'verse' sometimes implies writing that rhymes and has a rhythm, but perhaps lacks the merit of real poetry.
VERISIMILITUDE	truth-like; giving a strong sense of reality.

VERSE PARAGRAPH   a group of lines of poetry forming a section of a poem, the length of the unit being determined by the sense rather than a particular stanza pattern.

VOLTA   the Italian term for the 'turn' in the argument or mood of a sonnet which normally occurs in the ninth line at the start of the sestet, but sometimes in Shakespearean sonnets is delayed until the final couplet.

WIT   a general term which covers the idea of intelligence, but refers in poetry more specifically to verbal ingenuity and cleverness.

Printed in Great Britain
by Amazon

83206613R00132